W aro Osmoth ɪley and the Cleveland Hills

By

Keven Shevels

TRAIL GUIDES
p u b l i c a t i o n s

First published in Great Britain in 2013 by Trailguides Limited.
www.trailguides.co.uk

ISBN 978-1-905444-56-4

The route diagrams in this book are based upon 1925-1940 Ordnance Survey One-Inch maps updated by field trips and site visits.

Trailguides Limited
35 Carmel Road South
Darlington
Co Durham DL3 8DQ

Cover design by Steve Gustard

CONTENTS

Cover photos.
Front. Approaching a Cleveland Way signpost above Scarth Nick. Walk 4 Lady's Chapel and the Hambleton Drove Road.   Back cover. One of the Nine Stones. Walk 2 The Stones of Thimbleby Moor.

INTRODUCTION

1. Introduction

Holding a slightly elevated position on the western edge of the North York Moors National Park, Osmotherley is a picturesque little village comprised of stone built cottages. With the Cleveland Hills to the north and the Hambleton Hills to the south, the village is surrounded by moors and pastureland.

This close affinity with both hill and pasture ensured that the early development of the settlement was closely linked with agriculture. The marketplace being used for sheep and cattle sales until fairly recently.

However, it's name provides evidence of a mixed ancestry. In the Domesday Book of 1086 the village's name was recorded as 'Asmundrelac'. The first element of the name betraying it's Viking heritage coming from the Scandinavian personal name Asmundr, while the second element originated in the Old English word 'leah' meaning clearing. The clearing in the woods owned by Asmundr.

For those with an interest in archaeology and the past, the area surrounding Osmotherley, as with large chunks of the North York Moors, can provide fascinating insights into the distant past. Although partially settled during the New Stone Age, or Neolithic as it is more often known, over 4,000 years ago it was during the succeeding Bronze Age when the Moors were principally settled. A very favourable climate, more so than today, enabled the settlement and development of agriculture across even the tops of the high moors. By the end of the Bronze Age and the start of the Iron Age the climate had changed making it much harder for the Celtic tribesmen to eke out a living on the hills. If you know where to look there are still reminders of these past ages scattered amongst the hills and valleys that border this western edge of the Moors.

Despite it's long association with farming, by the 18th and 19th centuries Osmotherley was also a thriving industrial centre. So much so that in the period 1800-30 the population doubled from 500 to over 1,000 and many of the attractive stone cottages in the village were built to house these workers. This growth in population was fuelled by a boom in the local alum quarries and jet mines, activities which developed throughout the moors due to the underlying rocks and shales. The waters of the nearby Cod Beck also provided the motive force for a number of mills for the weaving and bleaching industry. Today's youth hostel, tucked away on the northern outskirts of the village being sited in an old converted mill.

Nowadays Osmotherley is a very popular tourist destination with many visitors being walkers and cyclists attracted to the area by it's natural beauty. This is further enhanced by the fact that the Cleveland Way, one of our most popular long distance national trails, passes right through the village. In addition to this our most popular long distance walk, Wainwright's Coast to Coast walk, starts it's climb up onto the North York Moors not too far from Osmotherley. But not to be outdone, the Moor's own long distance challenge, the 42 mile (67 km) Lyke Wake Walk, starts outside the village close to the Cod Beck reservoir, the starting point is passed on Walk 6 Above the Cod Beck.

2. Access & the Right to Roam

The North York Moors are the largest expanse of heather moorland in the country and, as a result, a prime grouse shooting area. In the past access to these moors has been jealously guarded in order to protect the game birds and walkers have been restricted to public rights of way. A policy which has, in many ways, prevented the responsible walker from experiencing some of the best of the moors.

With the implementation of the Countryside Right of Way Act 2000 in 2005 and the introduction of the "Right to Roam" this has changed some of the access rights and certain upland areas of the Moors have now become legally accessible away from public rights of way. This legislation allows walkers the right to roam at will over "designated access land" without the need to be restricted to official footpaths and bridleways.

On the new editions of the Ordnance Survey Explorer maps, this new access land is marked with a light yellow coloured background and at the entry points to this land, the stiles and gates carry the new "access land" waymarking symbol of a brown stick man in a brown circle.

The details that accompany each of the walk descriptions will provide information as to whether the route uses rights of way or crosses open access land.

With the right to access has also come responsibility and the walker is expected to observe various limits and restrictions that are placed on their activities at certain times of the year. The landowner and/or farmer has the right to exclude access for up to twenty eight days per year and this is normally applied between May and early July to coincide with the breeding season of the ground-nesting birds on the moors. Where they are known, restrictions that may impinge on any given walk are shown in the details for that walk. However, don't take it for granted that these are going to be accurate as in each year these restrictions may change. Always check any notices that are placed at the access points for any restrictions. To find out more about out the 'right to roam' and whether any general or specific restrictions apply to any part of the North York

Moors then a visit to the website **www.countrysideaccess.gov.uk** will give you all the necessary information.

3. The Walks

The nine walks in this book have all been designed to explore the woods, hills and moors surrounding the village of Osmotherley while showcasing the landscape and history of this part of the North York Moors. The walks start both from the village itself and also from a number of different locations surrounding the village.

Anybody who has used one of my books before will realise that I have a little bit of a passion for history and how this is reflected in the landscape. As always this is shown within these walks as I quite frequently use them to visit and explore certain aspects of the countryside that I, personally, find quite interesting. I don't believe that walking guidebooks should be boring and, hopefully, the walks and associated notes will help convey my enthusiasm for our northern landscape to you, both as a reader and as a walker.

In the details preceding each of the walks there is an approximate time taken for that particular walk which includes a reasonable time to explore the various sites of interest that are visited. However, this can be variable depending upon how long you, as the walker, take to explore these sites. If you chose not to have a look and investigate then the time taken will obviously be shorter whereas if you linger and have a good mooch about then you may be longer than I have estimated.

The walks in this book have all been graded in accordance with the Ferguson Grading System ('FGS') and the actual grading is set out at the beginning of each individual walk to help you assess their difficulty. A detailed explanation of the FGS and how individual gradings are determined is set out on pages 107-109 in the Appendix to this book.

4. The Weather

Although the North York Moors are not particularly tall in comparison to the Pennines or the Lakeland fells, they are still high, open moorland and as such susceptible to sudden changes in weather which can present a risk for those walkers who are inadequately prepared.

In summer, when the sun beats down, this open rolling landscape can present very little shade. Therefore, in hot weather you should always carry sufficient fluid or drinks to avoid the risk of dehydration and if prone to the heat or sun-

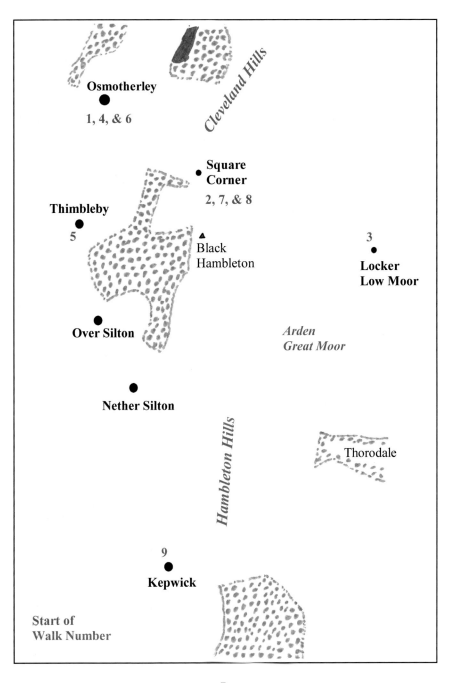

Osmotherley

1, 4, & 6

Cleveland Hills

Square
Corner

2, 7, & 8

Thimbleby

5

▲
Black
Hambleton

3

Locker
Low Moor

Over Silton

*Arden
Great Moor*

Nether Silton

Hambleton Hills

Thorodale

9

Kepwick

**Start of
Walk Number**

burn, wear a hat and/or sunblock.

In contrast, this same open landscape can offer little shelter from both wind and rain and bad weather can sweep across these moors with little warning. If rain comes, then this is often accompanied by a drop in temperature as well and even in high summer localised hail and snow are not unknown.

In the autumn and winter months fog and mist are also a real possibility, although the surprising fact here is that it can quite often come from the low-lying Vales of Mowbray and York to the west, creeping along the valleys on the edge of the escarpment and up onto the moors.

Looking at a map will show the position of the North York Moors as being adjacent to the North Sea. In most winters this usually makes them one of the first places to see snow in the North East.

Even on these low hills, it is important to be properly equipped when venturing out across the moors.

5. The Maps

Osmotherley and the area surrounding it lie on the western edge of the North York Moors. Only the one map is required for all the walks in this book and that is Ordnance Survey OL 26 North York Moors Western area.

The route descriptions included in this book are meant as a guide and although under normal conditions they should be sufficient to take you round the route, they are not intended to replace the use of the relevant map. Nor is the sketch diagram of the route meant to replace the OS map but rather to be used as an aid for you to identify the route on the map.

This countryside can be wild and rough, which is part of it's attraction, and at the same time the weather can be very changeable. It is very possible to set off in brilliant sunshine and then to find that later, low cloud and rain has come rolling in and visibility is very poor. The ability to navigate with map and compass is a required skill to safely traverse these hills and it would be extremely foolhardy to venture out with just this guidebook and no map.

6. Facilities, Tourist Information Centres & Websites

Osmotherley is a popular visitor destination and with being situated on the route of the Cleveland Way long distance trail, as well as being close to the start of the popular Lyke Wake Walk, it is well used to catering for the demands of the walker and other members of the outdoor community.

Within the village centre are three public houses, The Golden Lion, The Three Tuns Inn, and the Queen Catherine Hotel. All three double up as restaurants and can also provide accommodation.

Also situated around the market square are two cafes, The Coffee Pot Café, and the Osmotherley Boot & Coffee Shop. The second one, as it's name implies, being attached to an outdoor shop which stocks some of the top brands in walking equipment. Just in case you forget, break or lose any gear while you are in the area.

The full gambit of accommodation can be provided both within the village or it's surrounds, ranging from bed and breakfast, self-catering cottages and hotel rooms. An enquiry to the tourist information centres below or a quick search on the internet will provide more details.

Alternatively, the Cote Ghyll Caravan & Camping Park is situated a short distance outside the village. While in the same area, the popular Osmotherley Youth Hostel is located in a converted former textile mill on the banks of the Cod Beck at Cote Ghyll Mill just a ten minute walk away from the village.

There are no tourist information centres within Osmotherley itself. The nearest is located in the town of Northallerton, just nine miles away. The North York Moors National Park also operate a visitor centre at Sutton Bank on the edge of the moors fourteen miles to the south. Contact details of both centres are below.

Northallerton Tourist Information Centre
The Applegarth Car Park
Northallerton
DL7 8LZ
Tel. 01609 776864

Sutton Bank National Park Centre
Sutton Bank
Thirsk
YO7 2EH
Tel. 01845 597426
Email. suttonbank@northyorkmoors.org.uk

THE HAMBLETON DROVE ROAD

The Drove Road, also shown as Hambleton Street, Hambleton Road, Cleveland Road and High Lane at various points on the OS map, is an ancient routeway across the hills of the western escarpment of the moors. The use of the route may even date back to the prehistoric, there are certainly enough relics along it's length that date back to the Bronze Age and the earlier Neolithic.

From a point near Yarm where it crossed the River Tees, the road climbs the Cleveland Hills at Scarth Nick to cross Osmotherley Moor and then runs along the ridge above Cod Beck reservoir, past Chequers and Square Corner and up the shoulder of Black Hambleton. Continuing across Little Moor by Steeple Cross, High Paradise and Sneck Yate it reaches the top of Sutton Bank at Cooper Cross before continuing it's long course southward via Scotch Corner, Old Stead and Coxwold.

The Drove Road above the Cod Beck reservoir.

Prehistory ended with the invasion of the Romans and the start of their written history. In many parts of the country ancient routeways were continued to be used by the Romans albeit the old tracks were replaced by Roman roads. There is no evidence of this happening although the routeway seems to have continued being used, possibly by only the native people, well into the Dark Ages and beyond.

After the Norman invasion there is a tradition that William the Conqueror and his armies used the road during the Harrying of the North in 1069 where the

10

northern counties were put to sword and flame in response to a rebellion by the English nobles. By 1246 the route was being described as the 'Regalis Via', the King's Way, within documents in the Rievaulx Chartulary and the road was enjoying royal protection.

From the end of the 16th century up until the late 1800's it became one of a network of routes that were used to bring Scottish cattle down from the Highlands to the lucrative meat markets of the industrialised towns of England. In the days before refrigeration, meat was transported while it was still on the hoof and thousands of cattle, mainly Galloway and West Highland, walked down from Scotland. Travelling in vast herds the average pace was two miles per hour covering between fourteen and sixteen miles a day. The advantage of using this relatively high level route being that it avoided the toll roads that crossed the more populated and agricultural lands of the Vales of Mowbray and York.

Although the heyday of the Drove Road was during the 17th and 18th centuries it was also during this period that it received an alternative name. After the cattle had been sold in the southern markets, the drover then had to walk back home along the Drove Road laden with the proceeds of the sale to pass to his employers. Now he had to contend with the constant threat of robbery as he strode out along the Thieves Highway ………....

The Drove Road running along the edge of the escarpment after Black Hambleton.

Nowadays sections of the route are modern roads tarmaced over, while others are stony tracks and still others long stretches of soft springy grass. With the Road passing so close to Osmotherley it is perhaps inevitable that many of the walks in this book will utilise sections of it at some point during their length.

11

WALK 1: MOUNT GRACE PRIORY

Situated slightly to the north west of Osmotherley lies Mount Grace Priory, the finest surviving example in the country of a monastery of the Carthusian order. Now owned by the National Trust and managed by English Heritage, the site is open to visitors and makes an ideal subject for a walk.

DISTANCE: 2.5 mile / 4 km.

ASCENT: 515 feet / 157 metres.

TERRAIN: The route is mainly field paths and tracks with a section going through the woods surrounding the Priory. In places the path may be a bit soft and muddy. There is a steady climb back up out of the woods after visiting the Priory.

START: The Market Cross, Osmotherley. GR SE 456 972.

TIME: For the walk itself, allow 1 to 1½ hours. However, if you do visit the Priory then you can quite happily add another 2/3 hours, dependent upon how much time you spend exploring the site.

DOGS: As the route is on rights of way then dogs are allowed. Unfortunately they are not allowed into Mount Grace Priory itself.

ACCESS: This route is all on public rights of way.

Grid References

Market Cross	456 972
Path/track junction	453 974
Stile	450 980
Mount Grace Priory	449 985
Track	452 980
Market Cross	456 972

FGS Grading

Grading is T4 [D0, N1, T0, R1, H2]

Distance	0	Up to 6 miles
Navigation	1	Basic navigation skills needed
Terrain	0	75% + on graded track or path
Remoteness	1	Countryside in fairly close proximity to habitation – at least 80% of the route within 2 miles
Height	2	Over 125 ft per mile

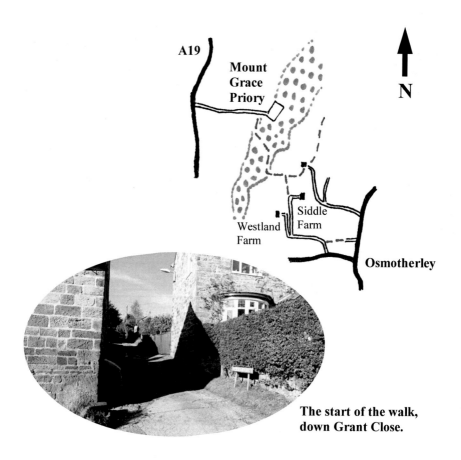

The start of the walk, down Grant Close.

THE WALK

1. From the market cross, head northwards up the main street and after a couple of hundred metres you'll come to a lane on the left side of the road called Grant Close. Turn left here to head down the lane and at the bottom go through the waymarked gate and then cross the stile into a field. Follow the hedge on the left to the end of the field, go through the gate and now follow the hedge on the right to a visible gate and stile on the bottom end of the field. When there, cross the stile onto a track. **GR 453 974.**

2. Turn right to follow the track and after just over 300 metres you'll come to a corner where the track splits although both branches turn right. Take the first turning right in front of the hedge and follow the track as it climbs slightly between two lines of trees.

Heading up between the two lines of trees and, inset, the junction where the track splits.

The track passes Westlands Farm, a short distance away over on the left, before coming to a gate. Go through and as you approach the buildings of Siddle Farm in front, the track turns right into the yard. Here, leave the track to go straight ahead through a waymarked gate and into a field. Now follow the hedge on the left to the end of the field where you'll find a stone slab over a small stream and a waymarked stile. **GR 450 980.**

3. Cross the stile and turn left to follow the side of the field downhill to visit the Priory. Afterwards you return back to this stile so it is handy remembering it. At the bottom of the field is a stile in the corner, hidden behind a tree.

Following the path down through the trees.

Cross this into the woods and follow the path as it bears to the right heading down the bank. At the time of test walking, forestry work was going on in the woods so after a short while the path turns into vehicle tracks as it goes down the bank. At the bottom the path turns right to follow a fence with an open field on the other side. Stay on the path, going past a gate on your left, to come to a footbridge and stile that lead into the left-hand field.

Cross and turn right to another stile a couple of metres away in the field corner that leads into the Priory's car park. Once in the car park, go straight ahead to cross a bridge over a small stream and then turn right to head up to the Priory itself. **GR 449 985.**

The entrance to the Priory.

16

4. After visiting the Priory it's now time to re-trace your steps. Head back to the car park and cross the stile in the top corner into the field and from there cross the stile and footbridge back into the woods. The same path that brought you down to the Priory now takes you back up the bank and across the stile out of the woods. Now follow the edge of the field uphill to come back to the stile on the right that you crossed earlier.

However, don't cross the stile but instead continue uphill to a visible way-marked gate a short distance in front. Go through the gate and follow the old track as it continues straight ahead and then bears to the left to come to another waymarked gate.

Go through but instead of heading for the obvious gate immediately opposite, make your way to a waymarked gate to the right of the farm buildings in front. Once through the gate, keep the buildings on your left and go straight ahead to a large wooden signpost and join a track there. **GR 452 980.**

5. Turn right onto the track, called Ruebury Lane, and follow it back to Osmotherley. Along the way the lane presents some grand views out from the side of the escarpment out over the Vale of Mowbray. On a clear day the summits of the Dales can be easily made out. After a little while the track up to Lady's Chapel is passed on the left. This place of worship is visited on a later walk in this book.

Continue on down the lane eventually passing a number of houses before reaching the roadside. Here turn right, to follow the road the short distance downhill into the village.

The view across the Vale of Mowbray to the Pennines.

17

MOUNT GRACE PRIORY

Lying to the north-west of Osmotherley is the finest preserved of the nine Carthusian monasteries built in England during the Middle Ages. Mount Grace Priory was founded in 1398 by Thomas de Holland, with the agreement of Richard II, as a place of prayer, study and contemplation for monks of the Carthusian order.

The order was founded in 1048 by St Bruno of Reims, who took Christ's wanderings in the desert as the example for his monks to follow. Unlike other monastic orders of the time where the monks lived and worked together, the Carthusian order followed strict principles where the monks lived like hermits to avoid worldly distractions, not only shunning the outside world but even avoiding contact with each other.

The monks, of which there were twenty-four including the prior, lived in their own individual two-storey cell with a walled garden to the back of it. Serving hatches next to the cell doors were cleverly angled so that meals could be passed to the monks inside without any physical contact between them and the lay-brothers who performed the day to day work of the religious community.

The reconstructed cell providing an insight into the lives of the monks.

Although today, most of the cells are no higher than their foundations, one cell was reconstructed and furnished in the early 1900's by the then owner. Today it presents a fascinating insight into the life of the monks all those years ago.

With donations of land and property, the priory became quite wealthy and at it's height the income generated from these even exceeded that of it's Cistercian neighbours at Rievaulx Abbey. However, the riches of these religious orders contributed greatly to Henry VIII's decision to disband them, a period known as the Dissolution of the Monasteries. Much of the wealth of the various orders being confiscated by the Crown.

In 1539 the keys to Mount Grace Priory were handed over to Henry's men by John Wilson, the last prior of the Priory.

The remains of the old church.

Nowadays the Priory lies in ruins, the best preserved part being the old church, the tower of which still stands at it's original height. Owned by the National Trust and managed by English Heritage, Mount Grace Priory is open to the general public, with a small admission charge. Access to the site being through a manor house built on an earlier gatehouse in 1654, with the house holding several exhibitions of the life of the Priory through the ages.

Surrounded by wooded slopes, the Priory is one of the most tranquil settings on the North York Moors and for visitors to the area, fully deserves to be sampled.

Gratitude must be given to English Heritage for allowing the use of the photos of the Priory.

WALK 2: THE STONES OF THIMBLEBY MOOR

In the last walk we visited a site of major religious significance dating back to the Middle Ages. On this walk you will visit another site of possible religious significance but this one being much, much older dating back to man's very early days on the moors.

Located on the northern end of the Hambleton Hills, Thimbleby Moor is a relatively small area of enclosed moorland covered with deep heather. The land rises to an area of higher ground hidden within the forestry plantations of Silton. Near to this high point is a group of standing stones known as the Nine Stones.

However, further down the slope towards Oak Dale lie a number of cup and ring marked stones. Unfortunately all but one lie on private land and are not readily accessible. But the one that is, is arguably one of the best examples of rock art found on the North York Moors.

DISTANCE: 3.1 mile / 5 km.
ASCENT: 217 feet / 66 metres.
START: Square Corner parking space on the moorland road from Osmotherley to Hornby. GR SE 479 959.
TIME: For the walk itself, allow 1½ to 2 hours. However, you can easily add on at least another hour dependent upon how much time you spend exploring the two sites.
TERRAIN: The first part of this walk is along a decent moorland vehicle track. The second part is totally the opposite involving a walk uphill across pathless moor complete with heather bashing and avoiding the odd "boggy bit". The climbing, although over rough ground which always makes it harder, is more long and steady rather than steep.
ACCESS: This route is all on open access land.
DOGS: Not allowed on the access land.

Grid References

Square Corner	479 959
Cup marked stone	470 959
Gap in wall	463 958
Nine Stones	471 953
Square Corner	479 959

FGS Grading
Grading is F5 [D0, N1, T2, R2, H0]

Distance	0	Up to 6 miles
Navigation	1	Basic navigation skills needed
Terrain	2	25 -50% on graded track or path, 50 – 75% off track
Remoteness	2	Countryside not in close proximity to habitation – less than 20% of the route within 2 miles
Height	0	Less than 100 ft per mile

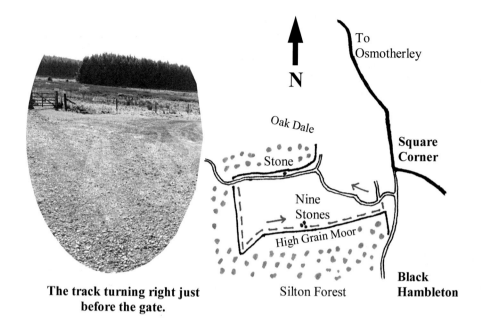

The track turning right just
before the gate.

Oak Dale

Stone

Nine
Stones

High Grain Moor

Silton Forest

To
Osmotherley

N

**Square
Corner**

**Black
Hambleton**

THE WALK

1. From the parking space at Square Corner head up the track that crosses the shoulder of Black Hambleton. Just before you come to a gate, turn right onto another track that heads over to a second gate a short distance away. Here you'll find a stile on the right side of the gate, climb over and follow the main track ahead ignoring the side track that goes off to the right. The track does initially climb slightly but then levels out and heads towards a line of grouse butts that can be seen in the distance.

Once past the butts the track descends before bending to the left and heading towards the corner of a wood. Ignore the turning on the right just before you reach the corner and continue on the main track passing to the left of the trees. The boundary wall of the wood, which in summer can be hidden behind the tall growing bracken, comes in from the right to run alongside the track. From the point where it first appears next to the track, it is approximately 90 metres to where two large stones appear on the right of the track lying between it and the wall. On the side of the second stone, facing the wall, are the cup and ring markings dating back to the Neolithic, four thousand years ago. **GR 470 959.**

ROCK ART ON THIMBLEBY MOOR

Rock art is a term used to describe markings carved into the rock during prehistory, in the British Isles this normally means from the Late Neolithic into the Early Bronze Age. A time period spanning nearly two thousand years, from 3,200 to 1,500 BC. These carvings are an enigma of the past, they are symbolic, abstract and the design of the carvings themselves is very diverse. Unfortunately the meaning of these symbols has become lost through time and although we can wonder and admire the artistry, dexterity and the imagination of their creators we can only guess at their function and meaning.

The use of this rock art appears to be multi-functional, it appears to indicate places in the landscape such as the siting of springs and other water sources, at the same time it seems to mark route ways on migration paths. It also features within burial mounds and seems to have a place in the ceremonial and ritual practices of the time.

Carvings were pecked out onto the rock surface with a sharp tool, usually antler, bone or another sharp stone. The markings themselves range from simple cup marks, a plain depression worked into the rock, to elaborate and quite decorative carvings.

The stone between the track and the wall.

23

Carved stones do not normally occur in isolation and are more often found in clusters or groups. In this case there are several known stones found on Thimbleby Moor although this is the only stone that is readily accessible.

The stone lies next to a modern track which tends to suggest that it is not in it's original position and may have been moved during the track's construction. It is highly possible that there may be other prehistoric stones and features still waiting to be discovered in the surrounding deep heather.

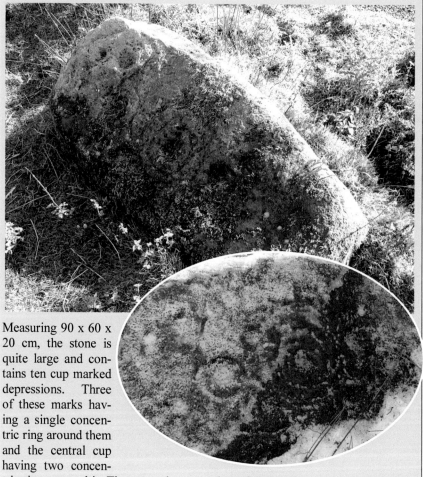

Measuring 90 x 60 x 20 cm, the stone is quite large and contains ten cup marked depressions. Three of these marks having a single concentric ring around them and the central cup having two concentric rings around it. There are also a number of grooves cut into the stone linking some of the cups together.

2. Continue on the track following the wall, a faint track comes up from the other side of it and crosses onto the moor but stay on the main track. Eventually you'll come to the rise of the hill and you'll start to descend to the woods below.

Cresting the rise of the hill.

Just as you start to descend a wall runs in from the left and the track crosses through a large gap in it. The wall next to the gap is a little bit dilapidated to say the least but is easily recognisable. **GR 463 958.**

3. Don't follow the track through the gap but instead leave it to turn left and follow the outside of the wall as it climbs steadily uphill. There is no path to follow and as you climb you do have to do a bit of heather bashing and may have to move away from the wall to avoid a couple of boggy bits.

However, stay as close to the wall as you can and when you get to the top of the hill you'll come to a wall corner. Turn left to follow the wall across the top of High Grain Moor. After 700 metres you'll come to the site of Nine Stones. **GR 471 953.**

Approaching the Nine Stones.

4. Continue following the wall as it slowly descends down the moor. At the end of the wood the wall turns right and the way ahead is blocked by a fence. Here you can turn left to follow the fence down to join the track at the gate that you went through at the beginning of the walk or, alternatively, it is an easy climb over the wooden part of the fence and then just 100 metres over the heather to join the Hambleton Drove Road. Either way you go, the car park at Square Corner is clearly visible and it is just a case of heading back to that and the car.

NINE STONES

On the high point of Thimbleby Moor lies a group of standing stones known as the Nine Stones. Often described as the remains of a stone circle, they may in fact have been more of a row of standing stones. There does appear to be some difference of opinion on this, although in either case it would still indicate that the site had some special significance to prehistoric man.

The northern pair of stones looking towards the north.

With many prehistoric monuments the setting is as important as the monument itself. Here you have a number of standing stones erected close to the crest of a small hill which is itself standing in the shadow of the larger Black Hambleton. Less than a kilometre to the east lies an ancient trackway, the forerunner of the modern Hambleton Drove Road, which must have been as important in the pre-historic as it was during the 17th and 18th centuries. To further add to the significance, the northern slope of the hill runs down into Oak Dale and scattered down it's slopes lie a number of pieces of rock art. There is little doubt that Thimbleby Moor formed a complex of monuments going back to the Late Neolithic or Bronze Age, over four thousand years ago. The extent of the complex being unknown as the forest to the south and the deep heather to the north may still hide many archaeological features.

The main features of the site are two pairs of standing stones, one pair to the north and the second pair slightly further south, close to the boundary wall of the forest. Both pairs of stones appear to have a fallen stone lying between them. It is highly probable that several stones have been lost or moved over the years. Work in the forest has revealed a number of stones that may have been part of the complex while it is also possible for fallen stones to be still hidden in the heather.

The northern pair of stones set against the bulk of Black Hambleton and, inset, the larger of the two stones.

Of the most northern pair of stones, the largest stands at about 1.2 metres in height and has a cupped top and weathering marks, eroded grooves which indicate that it has stood upright for a very long time.

The second pair of stones are set slightly further apart than the first pair but similar to those in having a fallen stone lying between them. There is another

stone close to these, set against the boundary wall but this appears to be a boundary stone from later centuries, part of a chain that follows a section of the wall, see photo.

The purpose behind the erection of the stones is unknown, so is the reason behind why this particular location was chosen. For these we can only speculate but for the people of the time to expand that much time and labour in positioning these stones then there must have been some significance that made all this effort worthwhile.

The cairn on Iron Howe.

WALK 3: ARNSGILL & COW RIDGE

A walk that follows two ridge lines across the moors and on the way discovers a mysterious prehistoric settlement full of stone cairns, over three hundred of them laid out over the side of the hill.

DISTANCE: 5.6 mile / 9 km
ASCENT: 755 feet / 230 metres
TERRAIN: Well-surfaced moorland tracks throughout with a short section of road walking both at the start and towards the end of the walk. There are two main climbs on this walk although neither of them are particularly steep, more long and slow.
TIME: 3½ to 4 hours.
START: Small roadside car park at Low Locker Moor next to the bridge over the River Rye on the road from Osmotherley to Hawnby. GR SE 511 944.
DOGS: As the route is all on public rights of way then dogs are allowed although they should be kept under close control. Livestock, mainly sheep, will be encountered throughout the route. There is a lengthy road section at the end of the walk.
ACCESS: The route is all on public rights of way. However, if you do explore the old field system on the descent from Iron Howe then you will leave the right of way and will be on access land.

Grid References

Parking space	511 944
Track junction	524 963
Track junction	531 969
Head House	535 971
Track junction	537 967
Cairn	530 953
Field system	528 950
Track/road junction	527 939
Parking space	511 944

FGS Grading
Grading is F4 [D0, N1, T0, R1, H2]

Distance	0	Up to 6 miles
Navigation	1	Basic navigation skills needed
Terrain	0	75% + on graded track or path
Remoteness	1	Countryside in fairly close proximity to habitation – at least 80% of the route within 2 miles
Height	2	Over 125 ft per mile

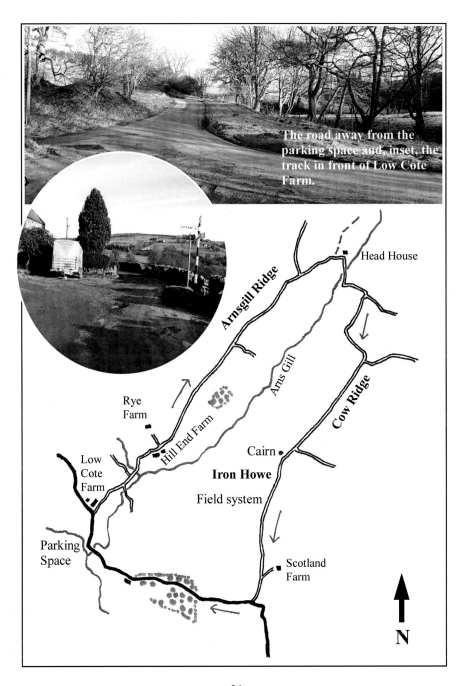

The road away from the parking space and, inset, the track in front of Low Cote Farm.

Head House

Arnsgill Ridge

Arns Gill

Cow Ridge

Rye Farm

Hill End Farm

Cairn •

Iron Howe

Field system

Low Cote Farm

Parking Space

Scotland Farm

N

THE WALK

1. From the parking space turn left and, ignoring the bridleway sign, follow the road up the bank to Low Cote Farm. Here leave the road to turn right and follow the track that passes in front of the buildings. There is a bridleway sign "to Chop Gate" on the corner of the left-hand wall, hidden by the bush.

The track now heads downhill, ignore the gate on the right with a bridleway marker on it that leads to a bridge, and go straight ahead to cross a bridge over the infant River Rye. Over on the right the water cascading over a fall between the trees makes a delightful sight. Once across the bridge, follow the track up the bank on the other side and at the top bear right to follow the bridleway marker to Chop Gate.

As you get close to the buildings of Hill End Farm you'll come to a marker post with a couple of yellow marks on it. Here turn left to go through the gate with the blue bridleway marker on. The track now passes across a short field to another gate.

The old lime kiln to the left of the gate.

To the left of the gate the remains of an old lime kiln can be seen. In years past nearly every farm on the moors had either it's own small lime kiln or access to one. Within the kiln layers of wood and limestone would be placed with the resulting blaze reducing the limestone to powdered lime. This would then be spread over the fields as a fertilizer to "sweeten" the grass. This agricultural practice is responsible for the characteristic moorland landscape of open moor next to green grassed grazing fields. Many lime kilns date back to the 1700/1800's, however, their use ended when an alternative, cheaper method of chemical manufacture was developed.

Pass through the gate and continue on to a second gate that opens onto the open moor. Continue to follow the main track and after a short distance you'll pass, on the left, the small quarry that was the source of the limestone used in the kiln that you have just passed.

After a couple of hundred metres the keen-eyed walker will notice the remains of a barrow on the right of the track (**GR 520 958**). The less keen-eyed, however, will have no problem identifying the tall, slender shape of the Bilsdale transmitter mast rising high into the sky. The sight of the mast is a permanent feature throughout much of this walk. The track continues above a small wood over on the right and as you pass, two minor tracks head away down to it, both of which you ignore to continue on the obvious main route. Eventually you'll come to a track junction. **GR 524 963.**

2. Ignore the turning on the right and continue following the main track straight on along the side of Arnsgill Ridge. After a short distance you'll pass a line of grouse butts with their white-tipped marker posts and a rough access track going off both sides of the main track. Continue on and you'll shortly come to another track junction (**GR 531 969**).

Take the right branch which continues straight ahead towards a small wood. Then, after a couple of hundred metres, you'll approach a wall and gateway. Here, ignore the footpath marker which points left and continue following the track through the gateway. The track is now a public footpath as confirmed by the small sign on the gatepost. Stay on the track to go down to Head House. **GR 535 971.**

Head House.

33

Now disused, Head House was the last farm at the head of this small valley. At the front of the building is a number of field walls including a small walled garden. The flat stones of this wall make a great seat to have a break and a cuppa with the sound of the stream running past just a few metres away. And the views aren't too bad either.

3. Continue on the track which now bears to the right to descend to and then cross the infant Arns Gill before starting to climb up the other side of the valley. Pass through a gate and shortly come to a track leaving on the left which you ignore, to continue climbing as the track bears round to the right. At the top of the climb you'll come to another junction, again with a track on the left, more white-tipped posts show the presence of a line of grouse butts not far from the track. **GR 537 967.**

4. Ignore the branch on the left to continue straight on. After a short while the track bends to the left to start climbing again up to the top of Cow Ridge. When you get to the top, the track turns to the right to start running down the ridge and here you'll come to another junction. **GR 537 962.** Again, ignore the left hand branch to go straight on as the track continues to follow the ridge passing after 300 metres, a minor track coming in from the right. Continue on the track heading towards the cairn on Iron Howe, which seems to rise from the ridge in front. Just before you get to the cairn you'll reach another line of grouse butts and two minor tracks going across the main track. Stay on the main track to the cairn. **GR 530 953.**

Approaching the cairn on Iron Howe and, inset, the cairn itself.

The cairn is made of loose stone and sits on top of Iron Howe. Howe is an Anglo-Saxon word and usually signifies the site of a Prehistoric Burial mound. This may be the case here as the summit that the cairn sits on has all the appearance of a weathered and eroded burial site of the Bronze Age, 4,000 years ago. In light of what you are about to discover it is a logical assumption that it is indeed a mound.

5. Leave the cairn to continue on the track as it now starts to descend down into the valley. After 400 metres a few piles of stones on the right side of the track start to give an indicator of the very extensive field system that lies on that side. **GR 528 950.**

Stay on the track as it heads slowly downhill passing as it goes a minor track on the right. After a short while you'll pass a line of trees and come to a gate and stile, cross and when you come to the tarmac access track for Scotland Farm down on the left, continue straight ahead for 200 metres to come to the roadside. **GR 527 939.**

6. Turn right onto the road and after a 20 minute walk, which is very pleasant itself as it passes through Birkwood, you'll come back to the car. As you walk along the road you will pass another lime kiln, very similar to the one passed earlier in the walk. This one lies next to the roadside and so presents an opportunity to inspect one really close up.

The lime kiln by the roadside.

35

IRON HOWE SETTLEMENT

One of the unique features of the North York Moors is the numerous groups of small cairns and burial mounds, with the groups sometimes comprised of quite literally hundreds of cairns. Located on many of the hill ridges, these groupings were constructed during the Bronze Age which was the time of the principal prehistoric settlement of the Moors.

One of the small cairns at the start of a length of wall and, inset, the detail of one of the cairns.

The cairns are mostly in the form of heaps of small stones, the heaps being rarely more than a few feet in diameter. To date little evidence has been found to suggest that they are burial mounds. However, they may still be connected with the ceremonies that tend to surround a burial but they could just as likely to be what are called clearance cairns. Piles of stones made by discarding stones during the clearance of the field before cultivation.

In the absence of any excavated material that can be dated, only a wide date range can be put forward for these cairn groupings, probably between 1,500 to 500 BC. Some of these cairn groupings also have a number of small fields and banks surrounding them, these fields and banks being characteristic of some Middle Bronze Age cultivation areas.

Line of a wall with another wall coming in on the left to form a corner and, inset, the line of another wall heading across the moor.

Situated along the ridge leading down from Iron Howe, this Bronze Age field system comprises hut circles, cairns, and a barrow, all surviving as earthworks. Low rows of stones in the heather show the walls of the field boundaries which are aligned in a rough south-west by north-east direction and which covers an area of around 9 hectares. Within each of the fields and also extending further south lie the small stone cairns, over 300 of them in total, varying in size from 3 to 5 metres in diameter. On the eastern side of the fields lies a hut circle, a stone circle representing the foundations of a stone built round house.

WALK 4: LADY'S CHAPEL & THE HAMBLETON DROVE ROAD

This is a walk that follows the hills northwards from Osmotherley and takes the opportunity to visit Lady's Chapel. Closely linked with Mount Grace Priory, the Chapel is one of the earliest religious houses established in this part of the North

38

York Moors and, surprisingly, is still in regular use.

The walk then continues through the woodland bordering the edge of the escarpment before descending over open moorland to the glacial channel of Scarth Nick before following the Hambleton Drove Road back towards Osmotherley.

DISTANCE: 5.9 mile / 9.4 km
ASCENT: 768 feet / 234 metres
TERRAIN: Mainly field and moorland path and track with a short section of road walking. A section of the track climbing up from Cod Beck is badly eroded but otherwise the tracks have a fairly good walking surface. Most of the climbs are gradual although the climb up the eroded section from Cod Beck is quite steep.
TIME: 3½ to 4 hours.
START: The Market Cross, Osmotherley. GR SE 456 972.
ACCESS: Public rights of way are used for most of this walk. However, a short stretch of permissive path is used to link Lady's Chapel with the Cleveland Way but this does not imply that this is or ever will be a right of way and at certain times access may be blocked. If you are uncertain about using this section then you can easily retrace your steps back from Lady's Chapel to the Cleveland Way and then follow that until you re-join the route proper.
DOGS: Are allowed on the rights of way. The permissive section is used by local dog walkers, however, please keep your dog under close control when on this section. Livestock may be encountered at various points during this walk.

GRID REFERENCES

Market Cross	456 972
Lady's Chapel	454 982
Path junction	457 990
Gates	461 999
Burial Mounds	469 001
Track/path junction	471 003
Road	472 001
Road/track junction	471 994
Road/track junction	473 974
Path/track junction	465 973
Track junction	465 970
Market Cross	456 972

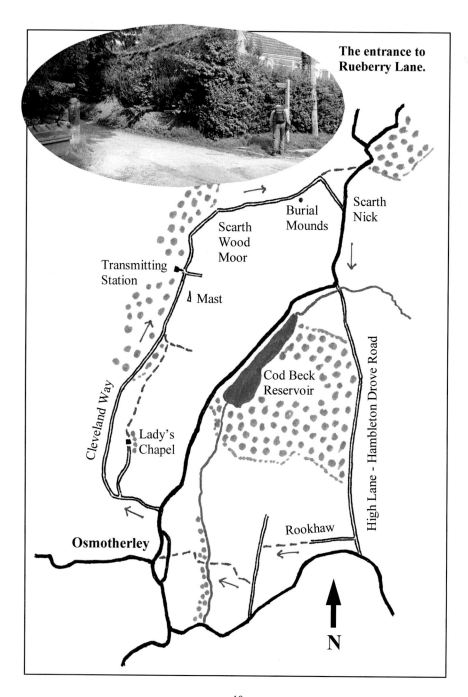

The entrance to
Rueberry Lane.

Scarth
Nick

Burial
Mounds

Scarth
Wood
Moor

Transmitting
Station

Mast

Cleveland Way

Cod Beck
Reservoir

High Lane - Hambleton Drove Road

Lady's
Chapel

Rookhaw

Osmotherley

N

FGS GRADING
Grading is T4 [D0, N1, T0, R1, H2]

Distance	0	Up to 6 miles
Navigation	1	Basic navigation skills needed
Terrain	0	75% + on graded track or path
Remoteness	1	Countryside in fairly close proximity to habitation – at least 80% of the route within 2 miles
Height	2	Over 125 ft per mile

THE WALK

1. From the market cross, follow the road called North Road, signposted to Cote Ghyll Caravan & Camping Park. The road climbs up and out of the village and when you get to the top of the hill there is a track on the left side of the road called "Rueberry Lane" with a Cleveland Way signpost pointing up it.

Turn left to head up this track, passing a number of houses along the way, and experience some stunning views out over the Vale of Mowbray. After about 400 metres you'll come to a junction with a track on the right, the track being sign-posted "path to Lady's Chapel".

The track, on the right, leading up to Lady's Chapel.

41

LADY'S CHAPEL

Lady's Chapel stands in isolation on a hillside terrace high above Mount Grace Priory. Surrounded by woodland, the spot is a haven of peace and tranquillity.

Built around 1515, under the instructions of Queen Catherine of Aragon, the chapel was also used by the monks of Mount Grace during the building of the priory. It is said that the flat terrace in front of the chapel is the resting place of those monks who died during this period.

Lady's Chapel and, inset, one of the pilgrimage crosses lining the access track.

Over the years the chapel has gained a reputation as a site of healing and a number of healing miracles are supposed to have occurred. Since it's early days this reputation has led to the chapel being an object of pilgrimage, an act that is still continued to this day. The crosses and quotes from the Bible along the access track being witness to these acts of faith.

The more modern house adjoining the chapel was built at some point after 1725 but later fell into disrepair. Both it and the chapel were restored in 1916 by Sir Hugh Bell, the then owner of Mount Grace Priory and the surrounding estate. The chapel is still an active site of prayer with a number of services being performed during the course of the year.

Turn right here to head up to the Chapel. After a short distance you'll pass the first in a series of fifteen wooden crosses that line the route, each marking a different point in the life of Jesus Christ. As you near the end of the track, where it bears to the right, climb a small flight of steps to emerge on to the grass in front of the Chapel. **GR 454 982.**

2. Go straight past the Chapel and on the other side of the grassed area see a small path going into the woods with a blue signboard next to it. Follow the path as it bears to the left for a short distance and comes to a stile which leads out of the trees.

Cross the stile and then bear right round a wall corner and onto a wide, rough grass track which follows the wall on the right. After a while the track approaches two gates, one after the other, go through the pair of them and follow the visible path through the field as it runs a short distance away from the fence on the left.

The view across the Vale of Mowbray.

The path heads for some trees in front where you will find a gate on the right hand side of them. Go through the gate and continue following the path as it shadows the trees on the left. As you get towards the end of the field the path changes direction slightly to make for a small wooden fence in the right hand corner where you will find a broken stile.

Cross the stile carefully and follow the path staying to the left of the wall. After a short distance the path forks but continue straight ahead next to the wall. Not long after you'll come to a junction with a wider path and on the right is a gate with a footpath marker. Don't go through the gate but instead turn left to follow the path away from the gate as it descends and bends to the right to arrive at a junction with the Cleveland Way. **GR 457 990.**

3. Turn right onto the Cleveland Way and follow it as it climbs slightly past some old quarry workings now reclaimed by nature. When you get to the top of the bank, you'll pass an open viewpoint on the left that looks out over the Vale below. Continue to follow the path as it makes it's way along the lightly wooded top of the escarpment.

The path along the top of the escarpment.

After a little distance you'll pass a radio mast in the field on the right before coming to a large, modern transmitting station. Go through the gates to cross over the access road for the station and continue along the obvious path.

The path now starts to give excellent views out over to the moors on the right with the distinctive cone shape of Roseberry Topping being clearly visible. You'll now descend down to two gates that give access onto the open moor. **GR 461 999.**

Approaching the open moor.

4. The path now makes it's way across Scarth Wood Moor and, being part of the Cleveland Way, it is wide, broad and easy to follow complete with, in places, erosion control paving. After about 900 metres you'll come, on the right side of the track, to a couple of burial mounds dating back to the Bronze Age, 4,000 years ago. **GR 469 001.**

Long since robbed out, these little stone mounds are but a shadow of what they used to be and act as a reminder of how

45

populated the high spots of these moors used to be in the distant past. Thought to serve a dual purpose of a burial site and a territorial marker, these mounds exist throughout the Moors situated on highly visible locations.

Continue on the track passing a fainter track that goes off on the right and within a short distance you'll come to a point where the track bends sharply to the right and a prominent signpost stands on the left. **GR 471 003.**

The track bend and Cleveland Way signpost.

5. Despite the signpost pointing the Cleveland Way straight on, stay on the track as it bends round to the right and descends down to join the road at Scarth Nick. **GR 472 001.**

Twenty thousand years ago, the valley of the Tees, over the ridge to the north, was one huge glacial sheet of ice pushing up to the edge of the North York Moors. As the ice melted, water became trapped between the front of the glacier and the escarpment forming a lake in nearby Scugdale. Being trapped, as the water levels filled the valley they gradually overflowed at Scarth Nick and formed this gap in the hills, known as a glacial overflow channel, through which the road now passes.

The name itself derives from the Old Norse, another indicator of the area's Viking settlement, word 'skarthi' meaning a notch or cleft, in this case in the hills. Although there is a modern road, this natural pass through the escarpment has probably been used since prehistoric times and was once part of the Hambleton Drove Road.

Turn right to follow the road as it climbs over the high point and then starts to descend, there is a thin path among the vegetation on the right side of the road which is a little bit easier walking. Eventually the road performs a sharp right hand turn and here a track leaves the left side of the road and goes to a ford and footbridge, clearly visible just a view metres away. **GR 471 994.**

The footbridge over the Cod Beck.

6. Cross the footbridge and follow the stony and badly eroded track as it makes it's way up the steep bank. The track passes to the left of the wooded slopes that lead down to the Cod Beck Reservoir, sadly at the time of test walking large swathes of trees had been fairly recently felled leaving a bit of an unsightly mess.

After a while the steep climb levels off and the surface of the track improves immensely. Stay on the main track, going past a gateway leading into the wood on the right and down to the reservoir. Not long after leaving the end of the wood you'll pass a footpath marker on the right and just after this the surface of the track changes to tarmac. Stay on what is now a road, for another 300/400 metres to come to a track leaving on the right side that has a chain stretched across it's entrance and a footpath sign pointing down it. **GR 473 974.**

STARFISH SF10C

As you are walking along the old drove road, on the left of the track, over beyond the field walls, lies the remains of Starfish SF10C. In the early days of the Second World War it was decided that there needed to be decoy sites to deflect enemy bombers away from strategic cities and other locations. Built in 1941 to distract bombers away from Middlesbrough, the Osmotherley Starfish was one of the first sites constructed and was one of six sites used as decoys for Middlesbrough.

The Starfish operated by reconstructing a series of controlled fires to simulate an urban area that had been targeted by bombers, the aim being to lure the bombers away from their genuine targets. Across the moor lines of fires were made using various methods from quick burning felt to creosote. The fires being lit as soon as the target town came under attack.

Nothing much now remains of the decoy site on the moor but the sharp-eyed of you may spot the control building still standing on the far side of the field on the left roughly at the point where the track turns to tarmac. Built of brick it stands behind it's protective earth banks although there is some erosion of the banks allowing a better glimpse of the building. As well as being the operations room for the site controlling the ignition of the decoy fires, the building would have also provided shelter for the decoy crew. Despite being relatively modern, the building is now a Scheduled Ancient Monument which reflects it's importance in our national history.

7. Leave the road and turn right to go round the barrier and follow the track as it gently climbs up to the brow of Rookhaw.

From the track the views across the valley of Oak Dale to the bulk of Black

The track leaving off the road.

Hambleton with the continuation of the old drove road seen climbing it's right hand side, are quite impressive.

Heading down the other side of Rookhaw.

When you get to the brow, the track bears right through a gate. Don't follow it but instead go straight ahead to a waymarked stile. Cross and then follow the wall on the left down the field to a waymarked gate. Go through and continue following the left hand wall past a gateway and down to the bottom of the field where you will come to a gate with a very prominent red warning sign about speeding horses. Taking care, go straight over the gallop, over the stile on the other side and onto a track. **GR 465 973.**

8. Turn left to follow the track downhill. This becomes enclosed as high hedges grow on either side. As you near the bottom and the hedges open out, a track becomes visible a short distance in front and just before you get to it, you'll come to a squeeze stile hidden in the hedge on the right and a Cleveland Way signpost. **GR 465 970.**

9. Turn right through the stile to join the track and follow it down to a second Cleveland Way signpost, the Way is now followed all the way back to Osmotherley. Following the direction of the signpost, turn right and follow the well laid -out markers as they guide you to the right of the farm in front and down through the fields and into the wooded valley of the Cod Beck. In the bottom of the valley, cross the gravel track and go straight ahead to a footbridge.

The footbridge over the Cod Beck.

Cross and follow the path on the other side as it climbs steeply up and out of the wooded valley. When you get to the top of the climb, leave the woods and follow the fenced path between fields and gardens to eventually emerge on a small lane within the village.

Go straight ahead, following a marker, down a passageway between the houses. This bends to the right and then emerges in the middle of Osmotherley opposite the market cross.

Heading up through Thimbleby Bank Plantation.

WALK 5: THIMBLEBY BANK & SILTON FOREST

A walk that can be very easily classified as a woodland walk as the bulk of it's distance is under the canopy of the trees. Although you do touch the open moor, it is only a brief touch which for a walk around Osmotherley makes a very pleasant change.

51

DISTANCE: 7.5 mile / 12 km

ASCENT: 1,273 feet / 388 metres

TERRAIN: Mainly woodland path or track. The outward leg follows a path that climbs up through the woods and plantations that line Thimbleby Bank while the return follows forest tracks through Silton Forest. The paths on Thimbleby Bank can, in places, be muddy and slippery and the descent into Oak Dale is both steep and rocky due to the path being badly eroded. Care needs to be taken on this section. Part of this route does utilise quiet country roads from the forest to the village of Over Silton. There is a steady climb on flagged stone path out of Oak Dale up to the moor at Square Corner.

TIME: 4 to 4½ hours.

START: Small roadside parking space at the bottom of Sandpit Lane. This lies on the southern side of Thimbleby, on the left side of the road as you exit the village. GR SE 448 952.

DOGS: As the route is all on rights of way then dogs are allowed but do keep them under close control. Be aware that this walk starts close to the Thimbleby Shooting Ground and if there is any shooting going on, then the sound of it can be heard very clearly at the start and finish of the walk. If your dog is nervous of loud bangs and noises then this may make this walk a little awkward.

ACCESS: The route is all on public rights of way.

GRID REFERENCES

Parking space	448 952
Gate	454 947
Stone	459 948
Fence & stile	462 956
Path / track junction	465 961
Footbridge	469 962
Path / road junction	479 959
Silton Forest entrance	480 954
Track junction	472 947
Road junction	460 926
Over Silton	451 932
Gate	454 947
Parking space	448 952

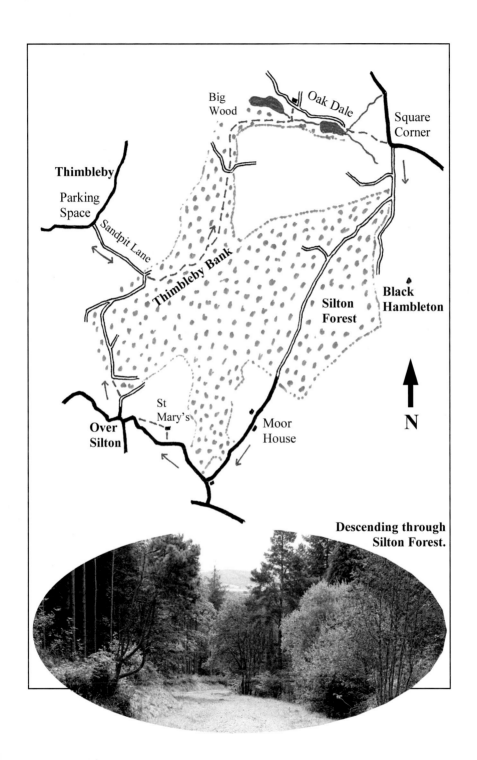

Big Wood

Oak Dale

Square Corner

Thimbleby

Parking Space

Sandpit Lane

Thimbleby Bank

Silton Forest

Black Hambleton

N

St Mary's

Over Silton

Moor House

Descending through Silton Forest.

FGS GRADING

Grading is F5 [D1, N1, T0, R1, H2]

Distance	1	6 – 12 miles
Navigation	1	Basic navigation skills needed
Terrain	0	75% + on graded track or path
Remoteness	1	Countryside in fairly close proximity to habitation – at least 80% of the route within 2 miles
Height	2	Over 125 ft per mile

From the parking space head up the left hand track.

THE WALK

1. From the parking space head up the left hand of the two track entrances. The right is the entrance to the private Thimbleby Shooting Ground. Follow the gravel track of Sandpit Lane as it makes it's way uphill, passing through a waymarked gateway and heading up to the woods that clothe the side of Thimbleby Bank. At the top of the lane you'll come to a waymarked gate leading into the woods. **GR 454 947.**

54

The three-way junction and the signpost hidden in the trees.

2. Go through the gate to be faced by a three way junction and a large wooden signpost partially hidden by the vegetation. Take the centre path, shown by the signpost as "footpath", and follow it up through the trees.

After a short distance the path bends to the left and here on the bend, a marker post on the right side directs you off the natural line of the path and on to a thinner path that goes up through the trees. The well-trodden path is easy to follow as it makes it's way along the top of a bank. The original sunken pathway is on the right below the bank, now boggy and unused. The path follows the line of

The path following the bank at the edge of the sunken track.

55

the bank as it shadows the sunken track until you eventually pass an old quarry on the right that can be faintly glimpsed between the trees. This is the destination of the old sunken way which now bears off towards it, the way being sunken by years of traffic going up and down to the quarry.

The graffiti marked stone.

The path continues straight on and soon enters a more open space of woodland where you will come to a large earth-fast stone marked by years of graffiti. At the moment the trees surrounding the stone are still quite young and so their tops don't interfere with the excellent views provided from the stone. **GR 459 948.**

3. A couple of metres after the stone the path forks and here take the left hand fork as shown by the marker post. The path now starts to descend down through the trees eventually passing between two large boulders before climbing a slight rise and then descending again before levelling out to run along the side of the hill. After a long while you will pass a marker post (**GR 461 952**) which will come as a welcome reassurance that you are on the right path. Continue straight ahead and you'll come to a fence and stile leading out of the wood. **GR 462 956.**

4. Cross the stile and follow the path straight ahead, the path then bears to the right to come to the side of a track next to a signpost. Following the direction of the signpost go straight over the track to a well-defined path on the other side. The absence of right of way signs on the track give a very strong indicator that you don't follow it.

A short distance into the trees on the other side of the track and you'll come to a wall, fence and waymarked stile. Cross the stile to enter the Big Wood and continue through the trees and the thickets of rhododendron. Along the way the path

Passing through the Big Wood.

passes a couple of waymarked posts, which is always a little bit reassuring, before turning to the right to run above the edge of Oak Dale. The trees here are a little more open spaced and over on the right you can start to see glimpses of the open moor which is coming down to the side of the wood. It's not long before the path joins a track. **GR 465 961.**

5. Turn right to follow the track, going past a small gate on the right leading to the moor. Shortly you'll come to a junction where the track bends to the left past a no right of way sign. Here, go straight ahead on the path heading for a marker post a couple of metres in front and once at the post turn left to follow the path steeply downhill. The path is both steep and rocky and for the main part quite eroded, take care as you descend here especially on the couple of sections where the path seems to go straight through the rhododendron bushes.

At the bottom of the hill the path bears to the right to continue descending but now not so steeply. You'll pass another waymarker before arriving at a footbridge over the Oakdale Beck. **GR 469 962.**

Heading down to the footbridge.

6. Go across the footbridge and follow the path to a small gate leading out of the woods and then from the gate, go straight ahead over the field to meet a track just in front of the house. Turn right to follow the track up the valley and as you reach the end of the house you'll pass two tracks on the left, one going into the yard and the other going up the side of the bank. Ignore these to continue straight ahead up the valley.

After a little while you'll approach a metal gate leading into Oakdale Upper dam, go through and continue to follow the track down the left side of the reservoir. When the track ends follow the path straight ahead into the trees to a footbridge which you cross.

The footbridge spans Jenny Brewster's Gill and the OS map also shows a Jenny Brewster's Spring. Jenny Brewster being, allegedly, a local witch.

The path on the other side becomes paved as it leaves the side of the beck and heads steeply up the side of the hill to emerge on the roadside next to Square Corner parking area. **GR 479 959.**

Looking back down into Oak Dale with it's reservoir.

7. Turn right to follow the track up the side of Black Hambleton, don't worry you don't go all the way to the top. Just before you get to the gate, on the left side of the track stands the Cray Hall Stone.

The Cray Hall Stone is a little bit of a mystery. It was discovered laid in the heather a couple of decades ago and was subsequently erected on the spot where it was found. The mystery being, where is Cray Hall ? There is no such location locally and a search of the County archives at Northallerton at the request of the discoverer also failed to find any place with this name.

The entrance into Silton Forest and, inset, the Cray Hall Stone.

Ignore the track on the right to go through the gate and shortly you'll come to a gate, stile and signpost on the right that leads into Silton Forest. **GR 480 954.**

8. Turn right here to enter the forest and follow the obvious main track, ignoring any side paths and firebreaks. After a little while, the track starts a long steady descent and soon passes a junction with a well-made track on the right (**GR 472 947**) but continue straight ahead going downhill.

At the bottom of the hill you'll pass one of the distinctive National Cycle Network mileposts and a small dilapidated building. Continue straight on and you'll go round a forest gate with the Forestry Commission car park over on the right. Again, carry straight on and the track now turns to tarmac, albeit with a long strip of grass down the middle - shows how quiet this road is.

There now follows a lengthy road walk but with the views of the hills over to

60

the left and the woods to the right, this is actually quite pleasant. After a little while you'll pass the house of Hunter's Hill on the right and not long after that Moor House on the left. The road now starts to climb slightly before, eventually, starting to descend past a cottage on the left and coming to a T-junction with Kirk Ings Lane. **GR 460 926.**

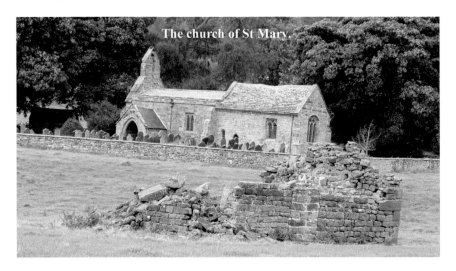
The church of St Mary.

9. Turn right to follow the road to Over Silton, passing as you do the church of St Mary standing isolated in a field a little distance from the road.

As you enter Over Silton go past the road on the left signposted to Borrowby and keep on till the next junction on the right. Here you'll find a no through road sign and another sign stating public bridleway Thimbleby 1¾ mile, don't be put off by the distance, it is definitely a lot closer than that. **GR 451 932.**

10. Turn right to follow the road through the village and when the road ends continue on the track. About 50 metres after passing the last house you'll come to a bridleway marker post on the left side of the track. Here leave the track to follow the direction shown by the post and follow a path that climbs steeply up the side of the bank.

Follow the path as it runs alongside some fields on the left and when it gets to the end of the last field it does a slight kink to the right and joins onto a forest track. Turn left to follow the track as it heads over and then down the side of Thimbleby Bank. You'll shortly pass a track on the right opened up by forestry operations but here continue on the main track straight ahead still going down-hill.

By now the woods on the left side of the track will have opened up allowing fine views from the side of the escarpment. Eventually you'll come to a wooden sign-

Walking down the side of the escarpment and, inset, the gate at the head of Sandpit Lane.

post where a track comes in from the left. Here continue straight ahead and after a short while the track re-enters the woodland. It's not long now before the track bends to the right and on the left side is the gate at the top of Sandpit Lane. Turn left through the gate and follow the lane back down to the car.

Cod Beck reservoir.

WALK 6: ABOVE THE COD BECK

The Cod Beck rises to the north of Osmotherley, formed by the joining of moorland streams. Unusually it then flows north to south forming a small valley that in some ways cuts Osmotherley, situated on it's ridge, off from the main escarpment of the moors before it makes it's way out into the Vale of Mowbray, flowing through Thirsk and, ultimately, joining the River Swale at Topcliffe.

The name Cod Beck probably comes from the Celtic word "coed" meaning woody and would have described the nature of the valley in days past.

This walk crosses from Osmotherley over to the eastern side of this valley before taking a circular route above the valley and up onto the moors where the beck is formed and then returning back down the western side to the village.

DISTANCE: 4.3 mile / 6.9 km
ASCENT: 653 feet / 199 metres
START: Osmotherley Market Cross. GR SE 456 972
TERRAIN: A real mixture of terrain underfoot on this walk. Initially the walk follows field paths before joining an ancient lane running along the eastern slopes of the Cod Beck valley. Woodland tracks and paths are then followed as you circle round the Cod Beck Reservoir before climbing up a well-trodden moorland path on the western side of the valley. The last section of the walk follows a green track and tarmac lane back down to Osmotherley. The route can be quite muddy in places especially the walled lane passing the farm of Rocky Plain and you do have to use stepping stones to cross the Cod Beck at the top end of the Reservoir, although at times of high water there is a footbridge across a little bit higher up the stream. There are two main climbs on the walk which can be considered to be more steady rather than particularly steep.
TIME: 3 to 3½ hours.
ACCESS: The route is all on public rights of way with the exception of the stretch from the road next to the Cod Beck up the side of the hill to join the Cleveland Way. However, as this stretch forms part of the Lyke Wake Walk it is quite well-trodden and defined.
DOGS: Allowed although keep them under close control. There is a strong probability that you will encounter cattle in the walled lane adjacent to Rocky Plain Farm.

GRID REFERENCES

Market Cross	456 972
Path/track junction	461 972
Gate onto lane	465 970
Entrance to woods	468 982
Track/path junction	470 990
Roadside	468 993
Cleveland Way	461 999
Market Cross	456 972

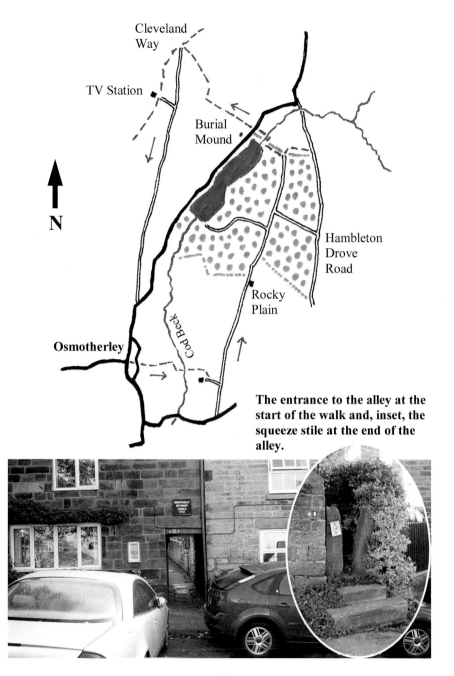

Cleveland
Way

TV Station

Burial
Mound

N

Hambleton
Drove
Road

Rocky
Plain

Cod Beck

Osmotherley

The entrance to the alley at the
start of the walk and, inset, the
squeeze stile at the end of the
alley.

65

FGS Grading
Grading is T4 [D0, N1, T0, R1, H2]

Distance	0	Up to 6 miles
Navigation	1	Basic navigation skills needed
Terrain	0	75% + on graded track or path
Remoteness	1	Countryside in fairly close proximity to habitation – at least 80% of the route within 2 miles
Height	2	Over 125 ft per mile

THE WALK

1. From the market cross go behind the War Memorial to see the entrance to a small alley. Above the entrance is a sign "Osmotherley Methodist Church 1754" and a footpath waymarker. Head up the alley and at the end bear to the right to come to a narrow lane. Go straight across and through a squeeze stile opposite and onto an enclosed path. This soon opens out into open fields although the path is fenced as it heads over towards a line of trees.

Once the trees are reached, the path turns right and descends via a long flight of steps through the woods to come to a footbridge over the Cod Beck. Cross the bridge and go straight ahead to meet a track. **GR 461 972.**

Cross the track and straight up the hill.

2. Cross the track and follow the waymarkers to go straight ahead up the side of the hill, passing through two gates as you go. After the second gate the path bears to the right to join a track above Whitehouse Farm. When you get to the track turn left to follow it to a gate leading onto a lane. **GR 465 970.**

3. Turn left to follow the lane uphill. At the top of the bank, go past the way-marked gate and stile on the right to continue following the lane. After a while you'll come to a gate with a stile on the left of it, cross and you'll find that the lane has now widened considerably. This stretch of the lane can be quite muddy and as you approach the farm of Rocky Plain, it can be churned up if the cattle have come in from the fields on either side.

Cattle in the lane as you pass Rocky Plain.

The lane continues ahead past the farm and towards the woods in front to come to a double gate leading into them. **GR 468 982.**

4. Go through the gates and into the woods, crossing a small stream and passing the ruined remains of an old building on the right. The track continues straight ahead and comes to a junction with another track coming in on the left and a rough firebreak on the right. Continue straight ahead on the gravel track and you'll come to another junction where the main track turns right. Ignore this turning and continue straight ahead.

After a little while the track opens up and gives a good view of the glacial over-flow channel of Scarth Nick in front. As you near the end of the wood, you'll

Coming to the end of the woods with Scarth Nick in front.

see a wall and ladder stile in front but just before you get to them you'll meet a path coming in on the left. **GR 470 990.**

5. Turn left to follow the path downhill through the trees. At the bottom of the bank you'll come to a well-laid out path that runs round the Cod Beck Reservoir. The reservoir itself lies just a few metres away on the left. Turn right onto the path and follow it for a short distance to exit the woods via a metal kissing gate. The path now crosses the shallow waters of the Cod Beck and goes up the slight rise on the opposite bank to come to the side of the road. **GR 468 993.**

Crossing the Cod Beck.

6. On the opposite side of the road stands a large stone marking the start of the 40-mile Lyke Wake Walk which travels from here, across the moors to the coast at Ravenscar. However, if you fancy visiting the remains of a prehistoric

68

round barrow which lies just one hundred metres away, turn left and walk down the road till you come to the first road-side sign on the right. The mound lies just a little way in from the road.

The round barrow just off the road from the road marker and, inset, the barrow itself.

Not a great deal of the barrow remains nowadays, it's proximity to both the road and the earlier Drove Road has ensured that it was robbed out long ago. Despite this, it is still very recognisable and it is easy to determine it's shape among the grass and heather. Probably dating back to the Bronze Age, this monument is one of a number along this stretch of the moor, most of which are hidden amongst the heather and more difficult to find.

The positioning of these barrows here on this low hillside next to the Cod Beck may have some connection to the prehistoric routeway that became the Drove Road. This may have been as a settlement, at the time of the Bronze Age this would have been prime agricultural land, or some form of boundary markers lining the routeway. Again it is thought that burial mounds often had a secondary purpose, that of marking out territory.

Return back to the stone marking the Lyke Wake Walk and follow the path behind it as it heads steeply up the side of the hill. At the top of the bank the path levels out and turns to the right to head towards the tree line in the near dis-

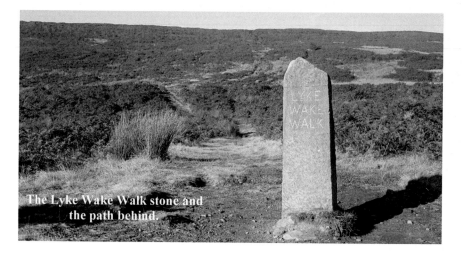

The Lyke Wake Walk stone and the path behind.

tance. After crossing a patch of boggy ground, the path arrives at a gate where it joins the Cleveland Way. **GR 461 999.**

To the right there are good views down across the moor to the isolated summit of Whorl Hill and the bulk of Carlton Moor rising in the distance.

7. Go through the gate to the large wooden signpost but don't go through the second gate. Instead turn left to follow the finger post marking the bridleway and follow the green track, keeping the wall on your right. After a little while the green track becomes a walled lane but continues heading down the side of the hill. It isn't too long before you go through a gate and join a tarmac lane.

The lane is the access road that serves the TV transmitting station standing on the edge of the escarpment that you encountered on the Lady's Chapel walk.

Turn left to follow the tarmac downhill.

After a hundred metres or so, if you turn round you can see the micro-wave transmitters rising over the crest of the hill on the right, looking like some giant science fiction creatures advancing over the top of the hill towards you.

Follow the tarmac lane as it descends down the side of the hill giving some very pleasant views of the valley of the Cod Beck as it goes, including the reservoir peeping out from it's surrounding trees. Eventually the lane meets the side of the valley road and here turn right to head back into Osmotherley and the end of the walk.

Whorl Hill and Carlton Moor rising from the mist and, inset, the TV transmitters "walking" across the hill.

71

The Victorian built Swainby Shooting House high on Whorlton Moor.

WALK 7: MILEY PIKE & HOLY WELL GILL

The heather clad expanse of the North York Moors is nowadays very closely associated with grouse shooting. Although hunting and shooting have always happened on the moors it was during the Victorian era that grouse shooting really developed.

Shooting grouse had been popular with the upper classes since the 1820's but became increasingly fashionable from 1852 onwards. At this time the Balmoral Estate in Scotland was bought by Queen Victoria and Prince Albert and their trips north brought about a craze for all things "Highland". This included grouse shooting, Prince Albert was an avid hunter and would go shooting every morning during his stays at the castle.

This passion for the grouse caught on with the wealthy English landowners and the weekend shooting party became a feature of many country estates. For a rich and privileged elite the provision of what we would now call the infrastructure for supporting this pastime, such as shooting lodges, access tracks, grouse butts, etc., was easily enough provided.

This walk takes you away from the public rights of way and runs along the light and airy ridges that lie just in from the escarpment edge. Here, high above the source of the River Rye you'll discover the remnants of the heyday of the Victorian shooting parties.

DISTANCE: 6.6 mile / 10.5 km.
ASCENT: 482 feet / 147 metres.
TERRAIN: The bulk of the route uses moorland tracks with steady gradual climbs. However, there is a short section of a couple of hundred metres in the middle of the walk, where the track ends and you have to make your way across open country to join a narrow path that, ultimately, joins another track. During this "rough" stretch you do have to make a descent through bracken to the side of a stream, in the height of summer this bracken may be shoulder high making it a little bit difficult to see your footing.
TIME: 3½ to 4 hours.
START: Square Corner parking space above Osmotherley, on the Osmotherley to Hawnby road. GR SE 479 959.
DOGS: Not allowed on the access land.
ACCESS: Most of this route utilises the access land that runs over Osmotherley Moor. It is only in the closing stages when you are following the Hambleton Drove Road that public rights of way are used. Many of these tracks have grouse butts lying alongside or close to them which means that during the grouse shooting season, and in particular August, then it might be better to only use this route on a Sunday.

GRID REFERENCES

Square Corner	479 959
Robinson's Cross	485 956
Road/track junction	490 955
Miley Pike tumulus	488 964

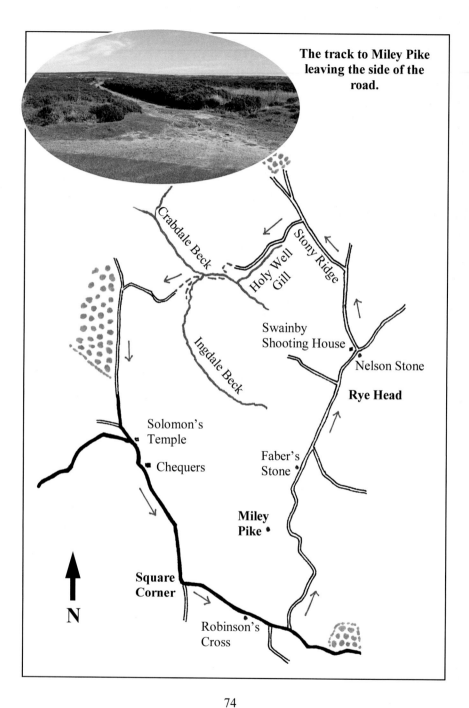

The track to Miley Pike leaving the side of the road.

Crabdale Beck

Stony Ridge

Holy Well Gill

Ingdale Beck

Swainby Shooting House

Nelson Stone

Rye Head

Solomon's Temple

Chequers

Faber's Stone

Miley Pike

Square Corner

Robinson's Cross

N

Track junction	492 972
Track junction	496 981
Track junction	491 993
End of track	486 989
Burial mound	484 989
Post	482 989
Post bridge	480 987
Wall	476 986
Track junction	473 986
Road side	474 973
Square Corner	479 959

FGS GRADING
Grading is F4 [D1, N1, T0, R2, H0]

Distance	1	6 – 12 miles
Navigation	1	Basic navigation skills needed
Terrain	0	75% + on graded track or path
Remoteness	2	Countryside not in close proximity to habitation – less than 20% of the route within 2 miles
Height	0	Less than 100 ft per mile

THE WALK

1. Facing the road from the car park, turn right to head away from Osmotherley and follow the road as it heads over the open moor. After about 700 metres, and as the road goes over the crest of the ridge, you'll pass the remains of Robinson's Cross on the right hand verge of the road. **GR 485 956.**

Although marked on the OS map as the remains of Robinson's Cross there is no remaining trace of a medieval cross or base. Instead stands this "modern" boundary stone, probably dating to the 1800's. It is at this point that the boundaries of Osmotherley, Arden and Snilesworth met. The stone carries the initial "M", possibly for Manners, the family name of the Duke of Rutland who, after the dissolution of the monasteries, became the new owners of Bils-

Robinson's Cross standing below Black Hambleton.

dale West Side. A second, older boundary stone lies fallen in the heather.

Continue following the road for a further 400 metres until you come to a track leaving the left side of it, just in front of a single tree growing on the roadside. **GR 490 955.**

2. Turn left here to leave the road and follow the track past a metal barrier and start the slow climb up the side of Miley Pike. After a little while the track bends to the left to go past the top of the hill and as it does so the tumulus and boundary stone come into view a short distance away on the left. It's an easy enough walk over the heather to the burial mound. **GR 488 964.**

Miley Pike tumulus is a scheduled ancient monument and is another example of a Bronze Age burial mound located on the top of a prominent landmark, probably acting as the dual purpose territory marker. However, you'll notice that many of the stones that make up the summit have been shaped and

Miley Pike tumulus seen from the track.

smoothed off, not at all like the natural stone used on these mounds. Long before it was declared a monument, the Victorian landowner built a stone shooting house on the summit of this hill. Now the top is a combination of the natural stone of the tumulus and the carved stone walls of the house.

3. Return back to the track and continue to follow it as it heads across the moor. It's not long before you arrive at Faber's Stone standing on the left side of the track.

Standing next to the track are two stones known collectively as Faber's Stone,

Faber's Stone.

both marking the estate boundary as it runs along the ridge. The older stone has possibly been here since the 1200's, it is in similar condition to the Nelson Stone which is encountered a little later along the same boundary and which is known to have been in place since that date. The younger, more ornate stone has been in place since the 1800's, have a close look at the markings, they are a fine example of the stonemason's craft. This and other similar stones will have been erected during the heyday of Victorian grouse shooting, newer, more ornate stones replacing the old, plainer ones. A sign of wealth, power and influence and even possibly just showing off to the invited guests of the shooting parties as they made their way past to the butts.

Shortly after passing these two stones, you'll come to a junction with a track coming in from the right. **GR 492 972.**

4. Continue straight ahead making for the distant shooting hut. After a little while you'll pass another track going off on the left and at this junction stands another upright ancient stone.

The unnamed boundary stone showing the OS benchmark.

Standing at the junction is another old boundary stone, this one being marked with an OS benchmark. A benchmark is an aid to the mapmaker and is cut into rock or stone, normally on churches or bridges. Things that are unlikely to be pulled down so it is quite unusual to see one on a boundary stone. The mark is a wedge-like horizontal notch above a broad arrow. The arrow being the sign of the War Department who originally controlled the Ordinance Survey. The mark indicates an ascertained height or level and when a Surveyor is "levelling" he would fit an angle iron into the notch as a bench or support for his levelling staff and would then work from this known benchmark.

Continue ahead to the hut and just a few metres after it come to yet another track junction on the left. **GR 496 981.**

Swainby Shooting House.

On the left of the track is Swainby Shooting House. Built during the 1800's this stone building provided the base for a day's shooting for the Victorian sportsman. Between drives, where the grouse were driven towards the guns by beaters, they would retire to the house for refreshments provided by the staff brought up from the lodge. The house is more functional than ornate, plain stone walls and no windows. It was not designed for habitation and no windows made it more weatherproof.

The Nelson Stone.

On the opposite side of the track to the shooting house stands the Nelson Stone. Dating back to around 1200, the stone is one of a number of old stones marking the boundaries of Whorlton, Osmotherley and Snilesworth. The name Nelson derives from Nelehou. For many years a Victorian stone, similar in carving to the one at Faber's Stone, stood next to the Nelson Stone but seems now to have disappeared.

5. Turn left to follow the new track and after a short while it passes a long line of grouse butts marked with black and white posts. Eventually you'll come to a corner where the obvious main track bears left but a fainter track and the black and white posts continue straight on down the front of the hill. Stay with the main track as it bears left to run along the side of Stony Ridge, the amount of boulders on either side of the track give a clear clue as to how the ridge got it's name.

At this point the views over the hills of Carlton Moor, the tree-capped cone of Whorl Hill and the Tees Valley are quite impressive.

Continue following the track to come to a junction with another track on the left. **GR 491 993.**

6. Turn left on to this side track and follow it as it climbs up and over the ridge

79

to descend into Crabdale. After a short distance the deep and rugged gully of Holy Well Gill starts to run on your left.

The meltwater channel of Holy Well Gill.

At the end of the last Ice Age a lake formed to the north in Scugdale, blocked in the valley by a dam of ice. Eventually the lake overflowed to the south, cutting the meltwater channel that we now call Holy Well Gill. The water would have flowed down Crabdale and into the Cod Beck valley. As the ice sheet continued to retreat away from the overflow then the channel would have dried up.

It's not long before the dolomite surface of the track ends (**GR 486 989)** but the track does continue as two wheel tracks through the heather.

Continue to follow the tracks and after a little while they stop descending to turn to the right and run along the side of the valley. Within a short distance you'll pass to the right of a small burial mound (**GR 484 989)** and then the track degenerates further to being just a thin path between the heather. Continue on the path making for a strangely shaped pile of stones that can be seen a short distance in front. When you get there, these turn out to be the remains of an old grouse butt, possibly Victorian.

Heading towards the old grouse butt and, inset, the butt itself.

From the remains of the butt, look over to your left, to the edge of the valley and see a wooden post standing amongst the heather. Plough your way through the heather to this post which is not as far away as it looks. **GR 482 989.**

7. From the post, continue straight ahead for a few metres over the edge into the valley to come to a thin but distinctive path through the heather that is running along the side of the valley. Turn left to follow the path as it becomes sunken into the hillside and then bends to the right to follow a small gully down to the side of the Crabdale Beck. During summer the bracken here can grow quite high and it is very easy to lose the path. It can also be a bit difficult to see where you are putting your feet as you bash your way through the bracken and down the slope to the side of the stream.

The stream itself is easy enough to step over but be aware that in places the bank has been undercut by the flow of the water. On the other side you'll find what is effectively a "mown" path linking white shooting posts. Turn right to follow this mown path downstream, there are a couple of wooden posts marking the route of the path.

Descending down to the "mown" path on the other side of the Crabdale Beck.

Within a short distance the Ingdale Beck flows into the Crabdale Beck and just before you come to this junction, the path bears left to come to a thick post bridge a little way up the course of the Ingdale. **GR 480 987.**

8. Cross the bridge and follow the thin path on the other side as it bears right and then turns left to start climbing up the side of the hill. After a short distance the path forks and here take the right hand fork to continue climbing.

As you climb the path develops more into a track and by the time that you crest the hill it is a fairly well developed track heading across the moor. The track heads towards a line of trees but before it gets there comes to the side of a wall. **GR 476 986.**

9. At the wall the track bends to the right, continue following it as it makes it's way round the outside of the wall to eventually join the Hambleton Drove Road. **GR 473 986.**

As the track follows the wall you'll notice that in places, the surface still retains stretches of paving. At some point in the past this track was more substantial but for what purpose we can only guess.

10. Turn left to follow the drove road, going past an entrance into the forest on the right and passing through a gate. The surface of the track does eventually change to become tarmac and after another 500 metres or so, descends to join the side of a road. **GR 474 973.**

The two old gateposts standing at the side of the road mark the entrance to what was known as Solomon's Temple. Now just stones laid in the field, this was a building erected by local eccentric Solomon Metcalf in 1812. It was noted for, and got it's name from, having images of the apostles, the sun, moon and the stars on it's walls.

11. Turn left to follow the road for just over 1 km back to the car park at Square Corner, passing the buildings of Chequers on the way.

Chequers Farm was, until it lost it's licence in 1945, an inn standing on the Hambleton Drove Road. For over 300 years this inn provided hospitality to travellers on the road. Tradition states that for 150 of those years the same peat fire was kept continuously burning in the hearth. For some years after the inn continued as a temperance inn and tea rooms but sadly no refreshments nowadays.

The line of a Bronze Age field wall amongst the burnt-off heather.

WALK 8: A CIRCUIT OF BLACK HAMBLETON

The mass of Black Hambleton rears itself up on the moors behind Osmotherley. Standing at 399 metres (1,312 feet) this is the highest of the Hambleton Hills and it's shoulder is crossed by a section of the old drove road which at this point also forms part of the Cleveland Way. This walk does a circuit of this hill and on it's way visits one of the many prehistoric settlements that lie on this part of the North York Moors. As a final "treat" there is an option of an out and back visit to the trig point standing on the high point of this sprawling hill.

DISTANCE: 6.4 mile / 10.3 km
ASCENT: 830 feet / 253 metres
START: Square Corner parking space above Osmotherley, on the Osmotherley to Hawnby road. GR SE 479 959.
TIME: 3½ to 4 hours.
TERRAIN: The bulk of this walk is on tracks across the moor although there is a section using field and moorland paths which, at certain times, can be wet and muddy. If you explore the remains of the prehistoric settlement then you will be walking off the path through the heather. The climb up from the side of the valley to the moor on top of Black Hambleton is long and in some sections quite steep.
ACCESS: The first section of the walk uses public rights of way but from then on the route follows paths and tracks over access land until the Cleveland Way is reached at the Hambleton Drove Road.
DOGS: Not allowed on the access land.

GRID REFERENCES

Square Corner	479 959
Road/track junction	488 955
Dale Head	495 948
Field system	500 947
Settlement	504 947
Wall and gate	507 945
Track junction	501 934
Track junction	491 932
Tumulus	481 942
Track/path junction	479 944
Trig point	481 946
Square Corner	479 959

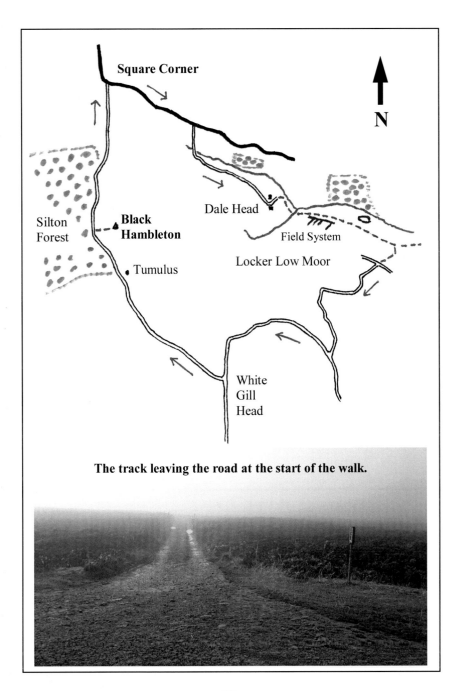

Square Corner

N

Silton
Forest

**Black
Hambleton**

Dale Head

Field System

Locker Low Moor

• Tumulus

White
Gill
Head

The track leaving the road at the start of the walk.

FGS GRADING
Grading is F6 [D1, N1, T0, R2, H2]

Distance	1	6 – 12 miles
Navigation	1	Basic navigation skills needed
Terrain	0	75% + on graded track or path
Remoteness	2	Countryside not in close proximity to habitation – less than 20% of the route within 2 miles
Height	2	Over 125 ft per mile

THE WALK

1. From Square Corner follow the road east away from Osmotherley for 1 km, passing the remains of Robinson's Cross which we looked at on the Miley Pike walk, until you come to a track on the right hand side of the road signposted as a bridleway. **GR 488 955.**

2. Turn right to leave the road and follow the track as it heads down across the moor to come to a gate. Once through the gate, the track turns to the left and starts to descend on the right side of a shallow valley passing a small wood on the opposite side. A little way after this and the track passes through a gateway to come to the ruined buildings of Dale Head. **GR 495 948.**

Approaching Dale Head in the mist and, inset, one of the ruins.

Walking North East

2014

Exploring the counties of Durham, Northumberland and North Yorkshire

3. Here the track turns left between the buildings and then right through a way-marked gate. The track now ends and becomes little more than a field path as it follows the fence on the right. As you cross the field you'll pass a marker post and just after it, ignore the gate in the fence on the right, bear left down to a large bridge over the Bawderis Beck. A waymarker on the left side of the bridge provides reassurance that you are on the right route.

Heading down to the bridge.

Cross the bridge and there is an obvious path going up the short bank on the other side of the beck and onto the open moor. Once on the moor follow the path as it runs along the side of the hill.

As with many parts of the North York Moors, this small area of moorland was home to a prehistoric settlement and the path runs right through it. It's not long before the shape of earth and stone bank walls can be seen on the right side of the track. The remains are easy enough to explore as they stretch up the side of the hill. Once finished return back down the hill back to the path.

Continue along the path but keep you eyes open on the left side, down nearer towards the stream. A couple of hundred metres later, you should see the remains of the settlement proper including at least one hut circle. Again, it just lies a hundred metres or so off the path so it is easy enough to drop down to explore and then come back up to the path.

Continue along the path to come to a wall and gate. **GR 507 945.**

LOW LOCKER MOOR SETTLEMENT

Compared to such as the Iron Howe settlement, visited on an earlier walk, the remains at Low Locker Moor have only been discovered relatively recently and, to my knowledge at the time of writing, have yet to be excavated. Therefore, there is fairly scant knowledge available that can help the interested walker to interpret what they see.

The settlement appears to be roughly in two halves split by the footpath going through the middle. As the path climbs onto the side of the moor, the first indication of the settlement is a line of low stone walls running over the moor on the right side of the path forming a field system. In appearance these are very similar to those on Iron Howe, however, these run up the side of the hill with cross-walls running along the face of the hill. As with Iron Howe, there are a number of cairns built into the walls at periodic intervals. The probability is that these are more likely to be clearance cairns rather than anything to do with funeral practices.

The first sign of the settlement, low stone walls on the right of the path and, inset, the wall in the burnt heather.

A little bit further along the path, on the left-hand side, down towards the side of the stream lies the remains of the settlement proper. As with the field system, here is a series of low stone walls but instead of dividing the ground into small fields, they form the foundations of a number of round houses and small enclosures which may have been gardens and animal pens.

Looking down to the settlement beside the stream.

The time period during which this settlement was occupied is not known although it is very likely to have been during the Bronze Age, similar to that at Iron Howe. The two settlements are in fairly close proximity and it is possible that the pair were occupied at the same time with frequent contact between the two. It is not unknown for Bronze Age communities to be in close proximity. and although as a time period the Bronze Age covered over nearly 2,000 years, it is known that once established settlements could be occupied for a considerable time span, sometimes lasting several hundred years.

Above, the stone foundations of a round house and, inset, the line of a stone wall.

4. Don't go through the gate but instead turn right to head uphill, keeping both the wall and a shallow gully next to it on your left. Even though this is not a right of way, there is a fairly well-used path making it's way up the side of the hill. It follows the wall even though it keeps a little distance away from it especially when it bears to the right to go round an old quarry.

After a steady climb the path comes to the side of a track which goes through a gate on the left. Go straight over the track to another track which runs steeply up Locker Bank. The path turns first right and then left as it makes it's way steeply up the hill.

Dale Head in the distance.

As you climb the ruins of Dale Head can be clearly seen below you. If you look around you, you can also see many features from the other walks in this book. Over on the far horizon the dark shape of Swainby Shooting House from the Miley Pike walk can be seen. Behind you the tall mast of Bilsdale transmitter can also be clearly seen, underneath it running down to the wooded valley is the ridge line of the Iron Howe settlement. Notice the fairly close proximity between that and the settlement in the valley below.

Continue on the track as it climbs up the hill, passing a side track on the left as you go. When you come to the top of the bank the track arrives at a junction. **GR 501 934.**

5. Turn right to follow the track as it makes it's way along the edge of the escarpment before it starts to turn to the left to head across the moor. As the track turns, you will be able to see straight ahead the small, square shape in the far distance of the Ordnance Survey trig point on the high point of Black Hambleton.

The track cuts across a narrow strip of moor between the upper reaches of Ryedale and the western edge of the Moors. It continues to bear round to the left until it ultimately joins the Hambleton Drove Road, now part of the Cleveland Way, at White Gill Head. **GR 491 932.**

6. Turn right onto the old road and follow it as it slowly climbs to run along the edge of Black Hambleton. After a while you'll approach the edge of Silton Forest on the slopes to your left. A boundary wall that joins the other side of the wall on your left provides a good reference point. Here on the right side of the track can be seen the raised mound of a tumulus. **GR 481 942.**

A tumulus is another name for a prehistoric burial mound, normally situated on the top of a prominent vantage point. Although the mound has long since been robbed out, two large prominent excavations testify to that, it is still worth a wander over to it for the views that it's location gives.

Continue along the track and it's not long before you come to a path leading off on the right side of it, a stone cairn also lies just a few metres beyond it. **GR 479 944.**

91

The turn-off to the trig point and, inset, the trig point itself.

7. A quick out and back trip to the trig point now follows, after all it would be a bit of a shame not to visit the high spot of Black Hambleton now that you are so close. So leave the main track and turn right to follow the path for a couple of hundred metres to come to the stone built trig. **GR 481 946.**

The views from the column are a little bit disappointing, Black Hambleton is a large bulk of a hill with a fairly wide, flat top which prohibits any scenic panoramas. But it's always good to say that you visited the top.

Return back to the main track via the same path that you came to the trig on.

8. Once back at the main track, turn right to follow it as it now starts to descend. The track is now followed all the way down to Square Corner, the car park and the car.

BLACK HAMBLETON

Standing at 1,312 feet (399 metres), Black Hambleton is the highest and most northerly of the Hambleton Hills. It is also the summit from which the range of hills take their name.

The name Hambleton comes from the Old English "hamel" meaning maimed in the sense of scarred or injured plus the word "dun" meaning hill, the Scarred Hill. As most of this range of hills have flat tops as opposed to a distinctive peak then this may have led to them being considered maimed.

92

Looking down into Thorogill with the reservoir peeping between the bare autumn trees.

WALK 9: A STROLL OVER TO THORODALE

Osmotherley lies at the point where the Cleveland Hills meet the gentler, rolling Hambleton Hills. Unlike the more northern hills, those of the Hambletons are built on a bed of limestone and this well-drained rock gives rise to a thin but fertile brown soil which in many places supports a natural, pastoral farmland even on the higher slopes.

This walk starts just a little to the south of Osmotherley, at the small village of

Kepwick and presents just a small example of the glorious walking that the Hambleton Hills can offer. Along the way it also takes the opportunity to explore artefacts from three ages in the development of man, the Neolithic, the Bronze Age and the Iron Age. Time periods in which humans left an indelible mark on the landscape of these moors.

DISTANCE: 8.4 mile (13.5 km)

ASCENT: 896 feet (273 metres)

TERRAIN: A complete mix ranging from field path and track, forest path and track to moorland path and tracks. There is even a section of walking across rough open moorland when exploring the long barrow. There is one long climb at the beginning of the walk that can be steep in places as it goes up an eroded gully. Later on your steps are retraced back down this gully. There is one section that passes through an area of scrubby woodland that is always wet and muddy no matter what time of year that you use it.

TIME: 4¾ to 5¼ hours

START: Kepwick. The small car park next to the church as you approach the village from the west. GR SE 467 909.

DOGS: Allowed on the public rights of way although keep them under close control. Sheep will be encountered throughout most of this route.

ACCESS: The route is all on public rights of way with the exception of when you are exploring the long barrow, trig point and tumuli on Little Moor and here you are on public access land.

GRID REFERENCES

Car park	467 909
Road/bridleway junction	466 908
Gate	475 902
Gate	485 900
Track junction	495 901
Track junction	505 890
Path/track junction	511 900
Gate	511 902
Track junction	511 905
Track junction	489 915
Track/path junction	489 909
Long barrow	492 903
Trig point	489 904
Gate	485 900

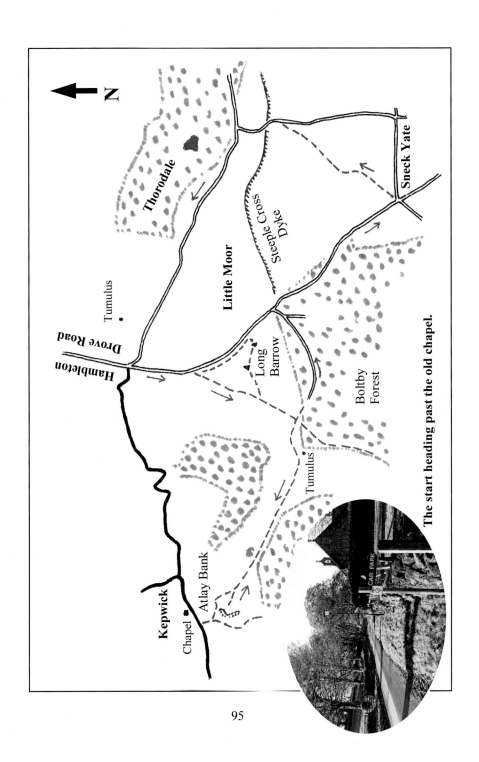

The start heading past the old chapel.

| Path junction | 470 904 |
| Car park | 467 909 |

FGS GRADING
Grading is F5 [D1, N1, T1, R1, H1]

Distance	1	6 – 12 miles
Navigation	1	Basic navigation skills needed
Terrain	1	50 – 75% on graded track or path, 25 – 50% off track
Remoteness	1	Countryside in fairly close proximity to habitation – at least 80% of the route within 2 miles
Height	1	Over 100 ft per mile

THE WALK

1. Exit the car park and turn right to walk past the church and out of the village. After just over 100 metres you'll come to a white gate and a bridleway sign on the left side of the road, there is also a footpath sign on the right side of the road so don't get confused. **GR 466 908.**

Through the white gate and follow the left side of the trees.

2. Leave the road to go through the white gate. The sunken way of the old route of the bridleway is obvious as it goes straight up the side of the hill but this is now overgrown and quite boggy. So instead follow the left side of it, keeping to the left of the trees and make your way uphill over the field to come to a stone wall at the top. Here turn right for a few metres to come to a wooden gate with a blue arrow bridleway marker on it.

Go through the gate and follow the path as it starts to bear to the left to run underneath the crags of Atlay Bank. The path climbs quite steeply and is normally quite muddy and in places quite eroded. After a little while the path starts to go up a steep sided gully and as you get into it's upper reaches this becomes lined with rhododendron bushes. Quite a spectacular sight when in bloom and not one encountered often on the North York Moors.

Following the path through the rhododendron bushes.

At the top of the bank, Pen Hill, the landscape opens out onto a small plateau and here follow the green path straight ahead towards a small group of trees. The path actually goes to the right of these and then runs alongside the wall bordering the woods on the right to come to a waymarked gate. **GR 475 902.**

3. Go through and the path now follows the wall on the left. Here the path is very muddy throughout most of the year and there are numerous little side paths through the low hanging trees as people have tried to avoid the worst parts but the path does generally follow the left-hand wall. Eventually the path comes to another gate. **GR 485 900.**

4. Go through the gate and, ignoring the other gate on the left, go straight ahead. After a short distance you'll come to a waymarker post at the start of a much firmer path. Follow this path as it heads up the side of the hill becoming more of a forest track as it goes. The trees here form part of Boltby Forest which covers a large expanse of the side of the escarpment. Eventually the track passes another waymarker post and just after that comes to a junction.

Here go straight ahead and go round a metal gate to come to another gate where the Hambleton Drove Road enters the forest. The large Cleveland Way signpost also shows that this part of the old road is also used for this long distance path. **GR 495 901.**

5. Don't go through the gate but instead turn right to follow the track as it runs through the top of the forest. After a while the track arrives at a gate where it exits the forest into a wide walled lane.

Following the track along the top of Boltby Forest.

The wide lane with the old stone walls on either side are a good indicator of it's use as a drove road. Ample room for large herds of cattle and yet walls to contain and control them.

98

Continue along the lane for a further 700 metres until you come to a track corner where the track turns into the fields on the right. Here you'll find a waymarked gate on your left and an information board stating the location as Sneck Yate. **GR 505 890.**

Approaching the track corner at Sneck Yate and, inset, the gateway on the left.

6. Leave the lane to turn left through the gate but instead of following the obvious track on the right next to the wall, follow the thinner but distinctive path that is heading diagonally left across the moor making towards the distant mast of the Bilsdale transmitter.

Although narrow, the path is easy to follow as it makes it's way through the heather and even though it does change direction every now and again it does head in the general direction of the mast. After a while the path approaches an old wall which is not really apparent until the last moment and when you get there, you'll find a grass track running alongside the wall. **GR 511 900.**

7. Turn left to follow the track and as it passes a gate in the wall on the right, ignore the track that goes off on the left. As you go straight ahead, the track leaves the wall to bear to the left and descend down into a dip in the field where you'll come to a hidden wall and a waymarked gate. **GR 511 902.**

STEEPLE CROSS DYKE

As you descend into the dip you are actually going down into what remains of the Steeple Cross Dyke. Earthworks are notoriously difficult to date but Steeple Cross is thought to be Late Bronze Age or Iron Age. This large deep ditch is what is known as a cross ridge dyke, a ditch and rampart that runs across the width of the ridge separating the western side of the escarpment and the upper reaches of Ryedale to the east.

Starting at the head of the Lunshaw valley, the embankment runs west to Steeple Cross but during this stretch much of the earthworks have been destroyed by forestry in the plantations of Boltby Forest. From Steeple Cross eastward the dyke is fairly well preserved as it makes it's way across the ridge to Stoney Gill Hole where it ends. In total the dyke runs for just over 2 km in length.

At the section where the track crosses it, the main feature of the dyke is the single ditch 6 metres wide with it's depth being 0.7 to 0.9 metres below ground level. On either side of the ditch earthen banks have been raised 3 to 4 metres wide and 1 to 2 metres high.

However, the dyke does not stand on it's own but is part of what is known as the Cleave Dyke system, a series of linear ditches and banks that run north to south along the western edge of the Hambleton Hills for over 9 km. As part of this system there are a number of cross ridge dykes that run at right angles to the main north-south alignment. Steeple Cross Dyke is one of these.

The purpose for the construction of these dykes is not known. It is possible that they could be defensive, they do run very close to the Iron Age hill forts of Boltby and Roulston Scar, but it is thought more likely that they formed a territorial boundary, quite likely between different grazing areas.

Looking east along the bottom of the ditch.

Go through the gate and follow the track up the rise, ignoring the track that goes off to the right. When you get to the top, the main track bears to the right and then continues straight ahead over the field. When it gets to the other side of the field, you'll find that the track is now high above the small, wooded valley of Thorodale. You'll now descend over the crest of the hill and join a more substantial track that runs along the side of Thorodale Wood. **GR 511 905.**

8. Turn left to follow the track up to the top of the hill where it then levels out and makes it's way over the fields.

It's a little bit of a surprise to find sheep grazing in closely-cropped grass fields on top of the moors but this demonstrates the difference between the harsher Cleveland Hills to the north and these more gentle Hambleton Hills.

You'll soon come to a gate across the track, go through and continue walking through the fields to come to a second gate, this one marking the boundary between the fields and the open moor. Go through and continue following the track across the moor.

Approaching the open moor.

The track is actually an ancient routeway linking upper Ryedale with the villages to the west of the escarpment and also the Hambleton Drove Road. As you go through this second gate onto the open moor, the low remains of stone walls can be seen on either side of the track indicating that at some point it was a walled lane. Traces of these walls can be seen along the length of the track.

As the track makes it's way over the moor, over on the right a large mound, slightly greener than the surrounding heather, can be seen. This is a burial mound, probably dating back to the Bronze Age, and is one of a number that will be encountered on this walk.

Eventually the track completes it's journey over the moor and bends slightly to the right to meet the Hambleton Drove Road, here also used as part of the Cleveland Way, and to also continue on as a tarmac road on the other side of the gate. The open space, at the top of the road, is often used as car parking and, especially in summer, you will encounter vehicles here. **GR 489 915.**

9. Turn left to follow the drove road taking care to obey the road signs! Within a hundred metres you'll pass an old boundary stone on the left-hand side of the track, the opposite side of the stone carrying the marking CT.

Following the Drove Road past the road sign and, inset, the boundary stone.

Continue to follow the track for another three to four hundred metres until you come to a second boundary stone on the left side of the track and a gate in the wall on the right side. **GR 489 909.**

10. Turn right to leave the track and go through the gate. Once through you are presented with a route choice. The easy and most direct route is to follow the obvious green path that runs along the side of the fence in front. However, if you wish to explore one of the oldest known structures on the moors then a little diversion is necessary before re-joining the green path further down the hill.

So from the gate, don't follow the path but instead turn left to follow the right-hand side of the wall. Sheep trods and a small path make the walking through the rough grass just a little easier. As you follow the wall you'll probably notice a number of low earthwork banks and pits across the moor. The banks are obviously man-made although the pits may be natural shake holes, there is a lot of uncertainty about these landforms and who built them and when.

After a short while you'll see the distinctive shape of a large mound about 250 metres away over on the right and standing next to it, dwarfed by the size of the mound, a trig point. Follow the wall until you are level with the mound and then count 170 paces. At this point turn right and with your back to the wall, head across the moor for 90 paces to come to the grass and heather covered mound that is Kepwick Long Barrow. **GR 492 903.**

From the barrow head over to the trig point and it's mound. **GR 489 904.**

11. From the trig point head due west over the brow of the hill from where you should be able to see below you the route of the green path that has come down from the gate across the slope of the hill. Head down to join the path and just before you join it, you'll have to cross an old sunken way.

Over the years, usage on sections of this path have lowered it's surface to a

The old sunken way.

level below that of the surrounding ground resulting in these sunken ways. Once this has happened then the path tends to become wet and boggy, water being attracted to the lowest level, and the path is then moved to one side onto

KEPWICK LONG BARROW

Between the years 4,300 BC to 2,000 BC, a period known as the Neolithic or New Stone Age, there was a gradual change in the culture of the humans who inhabited these upland areas. At this time the hills were not the heather clad moors but rather wooded forests full of ash, birch, hazel and oak trees. It was this changing culture that first saw the movement away from the hunter-gatherer to a farming economy with it's more settled and organised use of land and the domestication of livestock.

Not many artefacts from this period of change survive but high above Kepwick a fragment of this Neolithic culture still exists in the form of one of the oldest man-made structures on the moors. Although there are several thousand round barrows from the latter Bronze Age scattered across the hills there are very few long barrows from this earlier time.

In a similar manner to a round barrow, the long barrow represents the burial method of the time but where it differs is in both the shape of the barrow and the burial practices behind it. The long barrow is an oval hill of stone and gravel quite often 30 to 40 metres long and maybe a metre or two high. Several individuals were normally interred within the barrow with the barrow being used for burials through several generations possibly by a family group. As the need arose the barrow would be opened up and the remains of the deceased interred within.

Kepwick Long Barrow stands on Little Moor as a long mound of earth now covered in moor grass. Running on a south-east to north-west axis, the barrow is just over 35 metres in length with a width of 10 metres and at it's highest point is just over one metre tall. When first excavated by Canon Greenwell at some point prior to 1877, it was found to contain the remains of five individuals. Other than two flakes of flint, no other grave goods were discovered within the structure.

ROUND BARROWS

Standing in close proximity to the trig point are three round barrows dating back to the Bronze Age. Of the three, the one actually standing next to the trig is the most complete.

Being younger than the Neolithic long barrow, the round barrow also represents what is considered to be a fundamental change in funeral practices. Gone are the communal internment of a number of individuals within the one barrow. Instead the burial mound changes shape and becomes more personal, becoming the resting place of just the one individual. And that individual being of some higher status or rank than the other members of the group, such as a chief or priest, to warrant the effort to build a barrow of this type.

Initially a circle of upright stones would be laid out and then the body of the deceased would be placed in the centre. In some cases the body would be cremated first with the ashes being placed in an earthenware pot. Once the remains had been placed then the whole area within the stone circumference would be covered with earth giving a distinctive raised shape similar to an up-turned pudding.

There are said to be the some 10,000 of these round barrows scattered across the hills of the moors.

drier ground and these sunken ways get left behind.

When you are on the path, turn left to follow it down and across the side of the hill to come to a gate in a wall. **GR 485 900.**

12. You may recognise this point as the set of gates that you came through towards the beginning of the walk. Go through the gate and turn right through the second gate to start following the path next to the wall on the right.

Over to the left standing out from the trees is another large burial mound, this one being quite conspicuous by it's size.

Now it's time to retrace your steps along the very muddy section, dodging amongst the trees to try and find the driest route. At the end of this you'll come to another gate.

From here the path goes straight ahead following the wall on the left, ignore the waymarked gate in the wall, to pass to the left of the group of trees. Not long after passing these, you'll come to a fork in the path. **GR 470 904.**

The fork in the path leading to the gully on the right.

Here bear right to enter the rhododendron lined gully and follow the path down Atlay Bank to come back to the bottom gate. Go through and turning right to go past the trees, follow the right side of these trees down across the field to the white gate leading onto the road. When you're on the road turn right back to the car park.

APPENDIX

Ferguson Grading System (`FGS`)

1. Introduction

The FGS has been adopted as a means of assessing the nature and severity of the various walks in this book and the abilities and equipment needed to tackle each one safely. The FGS was developed by Stuart Ferguson, a long time fell and trail runner, climber, mountaineer, mountain-biker and general outdoor enthusiast. In the opinion of Trailguides the FGS is the most accurate and comprehensive grading system for comparing off-road walking, running and mountain-biking routes anywhere in the country.

2. The System

Tables 1 & 2, set out below, are used in order to give a grading to each route. Table 1 sets out three categories of country that a route could potentially cross, together with a range of factors that would need to be considered when tackling that route. The three categories are, Trail, Fell and Mountain, and after assessing which category best fits the route, a letter, either `T`, `F` or `M`, is allocated to that route. Where a route does not fit perfectly into one of the three categories the closest category is allocated.

Table 2 deals with five specific aspects of the route namely distance, navigation, terrain, remoteness and height gain, and each one is allocated a letter, `D`, `N`, `T`, `R`, and `H`. Each letter is also given a severity score from the range 0-3 or 0-4, in respect of distance (`D`). The higher the number, the more severe the route. The five severity scores are then added together to give an overall score. The overall score is then put with the Table 1 category letter (i.e. `T`, `F` or `M`).

In order to show how the grading has been determined for each walk in this book, the five individual severity scores are set out, in square brackets, immediately after the actual grading. So, for example, Walk 8 A Circuit of Black Hambleton has a grading of F6 [D1, N1, T0, R2, H2], indicating that it is a Fell Category walk with a total severity score of 6. This is made up of the five specific severity scores, for distance (`D`), navigation (`N`), terrain (`T`), remoteness (`R`) and height gain (`H`), of 1, 1, 0, 2 and 2 respectively. The highest total severity score which can be achieved is 16 and the lowest total severity score achievable is 0.

The table which accompanies the grading at the start of each walk sets out the specific factors, extracted from Table 2, that need to be considered when tackling that particular walk.

TABLE 1

	TRAIL	FELL	MOUNTAIN
Description	Lowland and forest areas including urban, cultivated and forested locations.	Moorlands and upland areas which may include some upland cultivated and forestry areas plus possibly remote locations.	Upland and mountain areas including remote and isolated locations.
Height	Not usually above 1,000 feet but may go up to 2,500 feet	Usually above 1,000 feet, up to 2,500 feet and above.	Usually above 2,500 feet and up to 4,000 feet.
Way-marking	Usually	Limited	None
Terrain	Usually graded paths, tracks and trails but may include some off-trail	May include some graded paths, tracks and trails but mainly off-trail	Virtually all off-trail
Height gain	Limited height gain	May include considerable height gain	May include some severe height gain.
Effects of weather	Very limited effect	May be prone to sudden weather changes	Extreme weather a possibility
Navigational skills	None to basic	Basic to competent	Competent to expert
Equipment	Walking shoes/boots. Possibly waterproofs Food and drink dependant upon route.	3/4 season walking boots. Full waterproof cover. Possibly map and compass dependant upon route. Food and drink dependant upon route.	Mountain boots. Full waterproof cover. Map and compass. Food and drink
Escape Routes	Yes	Some	Some to nil

TABLE 2

Score	0	1	2	3	4
Distance	Up to 6 miles	6 – 12 miles	12 – 18 miles	18 miles +	24 miles +
Navigation	No navigation skills needed	Basic navigation skills needed	Competent navigation skills needed	Expert navigation skills needed	
Terrain	75% + on graded track or path	50 – 75% on graded track or path 25 – 50% off track	25 -50% on graded track or path 50 – 75% off track	Under 25% on graded track or path Over 75% off track	
Remoteness	Urban	Countryside in fairly close proximity to habitation – at least 80% of the route within 2 miles	Countryside not in close proximity to habitation – less than 20% of the route within 2 miles	Remote, isolated location	
Height gain	Less than 100 ft per mile	Over 100 ft per mile	Over 125 ft per mile	Over 250 ft per mile	

Notes to Table 1

Graded paths = Well established paths with a stable surface.

Escape routes = The opportunity to cut the route short and return to the start without completing the full course in the event of weather changes or unforeseen incidents.

The Author

Keven Shevels

Kev has been involved with outdoor sports since his school days when participation in the Duke of Edinburgh award revealed the beauties of hill and dale and resulted in him walking or running through the countryside of the North East and beyond for most of the last forty years. Many of these trips into the great outdoors being visits to the heather-clad uplands of the North York Moors, an area for which he has developed a great fondness.

Over the last six years, Kev has put pen to paper describing routes through the North Pennines that reveal his passion for both the countryside and the history that has shaped it and the people who live upon it. That, coupled with an in-built curiosity to go and view things that spark his interest, tend to result in routes that take the reader into new, undiscovered areas and reveal a history that may not be apparent from the outside. He is not ashamed to admit that he is one of these boring people who can sit and spend hours reading a map like more normal people read a book. His great delight is coming up with new routes that he can subsequently explore and investigate. All of this has resulted in an easy to read, informative style of guidebook that has proved very popular among the walking fraternity and received very favourable reviews in both local and national press.

Now Kev returns to one of his favourite areas, the North York Moors, and in this, the first in a number of books that he is planning on the Moors, he explores the area surrounding Osmotherley which stands at the point where the Cleveland Hills meets the Hambleton Hills.

The author having a break out in the Durham countryside.

Walking North East

Walking North East is the brand name for the walking publications produced by Trailguides and reflects the pride that we, as North Easterners, have in our countryside, our history and our culture. Based in Darlington, we are a small independent publisher specialising in guidebooks centred on the North Eastern counties of England. Our target is to produce guides that are as user-friendly, easy to use and provide as much information as possible and all in an easily readable format. In essence to increase the enjoyment of the user and to showcase the very best of the great North Eastern countryside. Our series of books explores the heritage of us all and lets you see your region with new eyes, these books are written to not just take you on a walk but to investigate, explore and understand the objects, places and history that has shaped not just the countryside but also the people of this corner of England.

If you've enjoyed following the routes in this guide and want news and details of other publications that are being developed under the Walking North East label then look at the company website at **www.trailguides.co.uk**

Comments and, yes, criticisms, are always welcomed especially if you discover a change to a route. Contact us by email through the website or by post at Trailguides Limited, 35 Carmel Road South, Darlington, Co Durham DL3 8DQ.

Other walking books from Walking North East.
At the time of publication the following books are also available but with new titles being regularly added to our publication list keep checking our website. All of these publications can be purchased as books or downloads from our website.

North Yorkshire.
Walking the Hills of Upper Swaledale.
Walks Around Gunnerside.
Walks around Reeth and Upper Swaledale.
Walking around Osmotherley and the Cleveland Hills

Northumberland.
The Cheviot Hills.
Walks from Wooler.
The Hills of Upper Coquetdale.
Walks from Kirknewton.
Walks on the Wild Side: The Cheviot Hills.
Walks Around Rothbury and Coquetdale.
Walks in Hadrian's Wall Country,

County Durham.
Hamsterley Forest.
The Barningham Trail.
Ancient Stones.
The High Hills of Teesdale.
Walks from Stanhope.
Mid-Teesdale Walks.
Walking in Weardale.

Have a look at our Facebook page - **Walking North East** for current news on ourselves and our publications. The page also contains news, views and articles on all aspects of walking within the North Eastern counties of Cleveland, Durham, Northumberland and North Yorkshire. Definitely well worth a look and clicking the Like button.

For those that don't have or want to use Facebook then why not subscribe to our monthly newsletter. Titled 'Walking North East' this contains the same news, views and articles as our Facebook page. Subscriptions are free with no obligation to purchase and can be made via our website at www.trailguides.co.uk . Previous issues of Walking North East can also be accessed free via the website.

Acknowledgements.

As always acknowledgements must be paid to my walking companion, Harry Manuel, who not only provides good company on the walk but also checks and proof reads my route descriptions as well as appearing as the 'model' on the occasional photo. The preparation of this book would be a lot harder without him. I've also got to thank Lyn, my wife, for having the patience to allow me to disappear on these little expeditions.

Finally, I must thank English Heritage and it's staff for giving permission to use the photographs of Mount Grace Priory. Obviously if you are going to the Priory, I think that you should walk but whatever mode of transport that you use to get there, then I would take the trouble to visit. This site is one of those rare things, an oasis of tranquillity in a very busy world.